THE Method

Published under licence by Brown Dog Books and
The Self-Publishing Partnership Ltd, 10b Greenway Farm, Bath Rd,
Wick, nr. Bath BS30 5RL, UK

www.selfpublishingpartnership.co.uk

ISBN printed book: 978-1-83952-710-4
ISBN e-book: 978-1-83952-711-1

Cover design by Kevin Rylands
Internal design by Andrew Easton

Printed and bound in the UK

This book is printed on FSC® certified paper

MIX
Paper | Supporting
responsible forestry
FSC
www.fsc.org
FSC® C013604

THE Method

**LEARN HOW TO CONSISTENTLY FIND
MORE WINNERS AND START BOOSTING YOUR
BETTING PROFITS LIKE NEVER BEFORE**

DAVE HORNE

BROWN
DOG
BOOKS

Preface

Whenever or wherever has there been a book published on horse racing that actually instructs you what to do in order to find winners... notwithstanding the crank theorists that might tell you to back the second favourite in the third race on the first Wednesday in the month, providing the ground is not soft, or some other nutter who finds a key that works for them? The most practical books on the market are based on form figures and very often tipsters selling their wares, and not much else. The reason behind that is because there is nothing else.

The whole horse racing industry must be based on form figures, but the form book is turned upside down at an alarming rate on so many occasions and quite frankly it proves to be unreliable, and yet that is all we have got... or is it?

The writer of this book has found a niche that he admits is as near to cast iron as you can get in sorting out winners on horse racing, especially for the beginner and even more so for the initiated punter.

FOREWORD

It is a strange world in which we live, which is full of other people's opinions.

Everyone has opinions; even if it's complete codswallop, it is still an opinion. The world revolves around opinions.

Politicians on one side of the fence, whatever party it is, have their own policies that are completely different from those on the other side of the fence. These so-called educated Ministers sit in the Houses of Parliament shouting and arguing at each other like a bunch of unruly children in a classroom, and yet they are elected to rule and run our country.

With all that accumulated knowledge they still make a mess of it, forcing their opinions on each other, and we as individuals have to give way to their perceived knowledge and leave them to get on with it, whilst we have our own job to prioritise and sort our own lives out, keep ourselves healthy, find work, find somewhere to live, and find the money to pay for it all.

But there is a huge difference between **Knowledge** and **Wisdom**.

Knowledge is the information and skills that are learnt or gathered through education, whereas **Wisdom** is having good judgement, experience, and knowledge, and therefore a state of being wise.

It is my opinion, if you accept that I am allowed to have one, that we cannot depend or rely on what we are told by others, but instead we must build a platform of our own to stand on and make decisions for ourselves. All of which brings us to the conclusion of why I wrote this book in the first place, or indeed why you bought it.

My very first horse racing experience was a trip to Brighton races with my father at a very early age, and ever since, I have had an inbuilt fascination for the sport and all that goes with it. Those strange little men dressed in their multicoloured shirts, jodhpurs and shiny boots, balancing on those magnificent beasts, running at speed faster than a steam train, was certainly an experience that I could not shift from my very young mind. I was fascinated by the whole scene and longed for a repeat experience that unfortunately never happened again until I was wage earning myself and around 20 years old.

Even before my trip to Brighton, horse racing was in some way part of my daily life.

Although I had two older brothers, it became my job every day on my way back to school to put my father's bets on with the old-fashioned street bookmaker, long before the advent of betting shops. He would write his bet on any piece of scrap paper, wrap the money in it and I would deliver it to the bookie, a fat guy wearing an overcoat, who stood in the church doorway out of sight of the bobby on the beat.

At first, I never knew what he was betting on. I simply wanted him to win because of the enormous relief for the family when it happened.

Dad had a good job in London's docks working as a stevedore earning very decent money, but he saw gambling as a way to have extra money and have some of those small luxuries such as a telephone or a radiogram or even a holiday, that some people managed to achieve during those hard years in the 50s.

All he needed to do was manage his income accordingly, which he never ever did. Instead, he was in the grip of the addiction that gambling carries, and our family never saw the extras that a win on the horses could supply. In truth his gambling did exactly the opposite and my mother, my four brothers and I were all subjected to his losses in one way or another. But there was the joy and excitement sometimes that we would all experience on those rare winning occasions, because the pressure was off, at least for a short time.

Of course, the rare and temporary winnings only managed to plug the leaks of his earlier losses, but nonetheless it played itself out at the time and gave some sanity to the reasons behind his gambling.

I was sucked into the same trap myself, because as a child I only saw one side to his gambling, which was the winning. I never realised the problems and hardship caused by the losing because I was living it.

So, to find a bit of that joy for myself I would secretly increase the stake on his bets by changing, say, a two shilling each-way bet, to three shillings each way. I would then have to wait for the evening papers to be delivered to the corner shop where I could cheekily check the results in the stop press of the Evening Standard. There was no other way at the time.

My second problem, of course, was how to work out how much I had to come back if the horse won or was placed, but fat Joe, who took the bets, understood what was happening and allowed it to continue.

I was, however, governed by my dad's selections and, considering he was just about the worst gambler I can ever remember, my family's lifestyle and living conditions continued and reflected that in every detail of our lives, as well as my own money being flushed down the drain along with his and his poor selections. All of which I accepted, for some reason or another, including the losses, and here was the gambler in the making.

What is so very important in all of this was the fact that I wanted the excitement of betting rather than the winning. I found a necessity to bet without the need to win.

I was ten years of age with absolutely no responsibilities or commitments, other than going to school and eating what was put in front of me. I did errands for neighbours and had a little earner buying and selling wood. I was actually learning to gamble with the small amount of money that I had, and accepting the fact that I was following exactly in my father's footsteps and getting nothing back except empty pockets.

Which brings me back to the politicians who struggle to supply the nation with clear decisive rules on going forward. I was effectively doing what I was doing on Dad's opinion. I never fully fell in with that analysis until very much later in life. I was unwittingly being groomed into a gambler, which everyone reading this book will understand to some degree.

The answer to the other question, of why you purchased this book, is rather hypocritical of the above, because your intention has been to find someone else's opinion that would be different from your own or otherwise endorse what you already know. So let me clarify some important points for you from what you are about to read.

I am not a tipster and neither do I ever waste my time reading what other people think might win a horse race. I have done enough of that. I do not listen to tips or get involved with them, let us be totally clear. I have no degrees or other such qualifications that would enhance my position as an expert on horse racing, I am certainly not a paddock judge or breeding analyst, neither do I have any other talents linked to horse racing that I could boast about. I don't even have any background in publishing or writing and for that reason I would hope you accept my rather crude handling of the written word and trust you understand all of what I put over.

I was, however, a heavy gambler who lost his money at every opportunity and kept on doing so until something suddenly dropped that was much larger than a penny. It was too hard for me to walk away from my addiction or maybe I just could not live without it.

Whatever the reason, I was silently suffering with it. Gambling became something like a heavy suitcase that I always had to carry around with me, all because of the initial road that I built for myself and kept walking it for all those years. That road had absolutely no foundation and undoubtedly there are many thousands of punters who walk the same road to nowhere.

No more, folks, it all ends here. **No tips. No opinions. No systems.**

Just practical and essential information that I am about to share with you, which will steer you away from the familiar but uncertain route that all gamblers tread.

I have tried my head off to be clear and honest and share with you what has transformed my life, and my financial position, for a great number of years, and by following the **Method** you will be sure to do the same.

Finally, I will tell you that it is no good sitting on your laurels, or anything else you choose to sit back on, and expect to buy the magic racing formula that does not exist. This book more than emphasises that often purchased philosophy of disappointment and, as you read on, you will realise that horse racing is a very enjoyable pastime that can also be very profitable indeed

You will notice throughout the book, with some of the winning experiences achieved by yours truly, that I have gone back a couple of years. Please don't think I am singing my own praises or feeling smug by highlighting something that only happened some time ago. I am not.

I am merely explaining in as clear terms as I possibly can, with just a few examples exactly how they happened, that give the reader that pinch of history and proof of how it all works. It also can be proven quite easily, and I sincerely hope you take the trouble to check for yourselves all that I have spelt out.

Contents

The Challenges

Welcome to the fascinating world of horse racing, where punters can ride the waves one minute and sink like a submarine without power the next. I know this because I have ridden those waves practically all of my working life, and before.

The many facets of the horse racing game are such a challenge that even the most skilful mathematician would not be able to fathom it out. We can speak about scientists who rise to the challenges of the world's medical and structural problems and achieve the most complex solutions with practically all that is put in front of them. We have astrological experts that tell us about things in another galaxy. We can even tell, to the exact minute, what time the tide comes in at any given position. Yet ask anyone, and I mean anyone, to pick the winner of a horse race and back it with any sort of confidence, in other words put their money where their mouth is, they find themselves on ice so thin that they need water wings before they take a step. Trainers do not know, jockeys do not know, so what chance does ordinary Joe have of finding a winner?

You must be wondering where I am going with this, especially with yourself buying a book on how to be successful on horse racing. I am merely emphasising, if you are not already aware, the many challenges we take on when we gamble.

W.C. Fields said that Horse Sense is the thing a horse has, which stops him from betting on people.

It is true that you cannot win money on the horses, or anything else for that matter, unless you have a bet, and the question is, where do you find the information to make your selection before you place that bet? And, more importantly, why do so many of us like to bet?

A punter's dream is to uncover the secrets of gambling and earn a whole heap of money from betting, but the reality is, and especially with horse racing, that millions of gamblers have been digging for the same treasure in the same place since gambling began, and more people keep arriving to have a dig in the same place themselves. It is about time for punters to start digging elsewhere!

Well, I am not only going to give you that shovel, I am also going to show you how to use it.

What you are about to read in this book will give you a whole new concept in the approach to successful gambling on horse racing without getting bogged down with technical data that no one wants to do, and to be truthful, most of which does not get results.

So many professional punters have tried to spell out information that they hold in their heads, they have articles on how to win that are sold to the sports papers and they walk around with their ass hanging out of their trousers.

It is the wise man who appreciates how little he knows.

Quite simply I need you to be clear that horse racing is not a science and cannot be treated as such. I have just spent the last 3 hours of my time reading the reviews on the top **horse-racing for-profit books.** There are quite a few out there and I find reading the reviews far easier than reading the books themselves because I am not spelling out my own bias or unbiased feedback, I am virtually quoting what many readers expect from a book that sells information on gambling.

I have concluded that most books written on the subject are very much a waste of time and money. It is also the general opinion in the many reviews I have now read.

It seems to me the buyer/punter comes in two types. The first expects positive information that will transform his life and his bank balance and thinks he can purchase it in a book. And if he is not successful, he is therefore willing to declare to everyone else what a complete waste of time and money he has spent buying the bloody thing.

The second is more realistic in his approach, and somewhat pleased and satisfied that he has managed to at least uncover some of his own longstanding pitfalls and found something positive and worthwhile.

A close friend of mine, who I used to play golf with, is essentially a non-gambler, but likes the occasional bet. He was interested in coming to the races to enjoy a day out and socialise with myself and a couple of other racing nuts. I introduced Tony to my pals when we arrived at Newmarket July course, the sun was shining, we had a beautiful lunch in the members' restaurant along with a few beers and a bottle of fizz before we got stuck into the day's racing.

I swapped thoughts with my friends over lunch and the day turned out to be a very successful one. I had four bets and backed seven horses, three of which won. My pals also had a very good day.

Tony was quite hooked and fascinated with it all. Even though he did not back a winner, he was full of it on the way home, asking all kinds of questions. Tony was privy to see firsthand how easy the horse racing game is. He saw wads of cash that we collected from the bookmakers, experienced the buzz and had a fantastic day out.

He phoned me more than ever after that, asking if I had any tips, or when was I going racing again. He told the guys at the golf club how good I was at picking the winners. I then had others giving me their phone numbers, asking me to give them a call when I had a hot tip. All very flattering.

Tony was the perfect example of a punter who wants to be in the know. He became intoxicated with the surroundings, the atmosphere of the racetrack, and most of all the easy way of making lots of money. He wanted a piece of the action, he wanted the insider knowledge that only a select few of us can access, and that is how he saw horse-racing.

Tony was not privy to the years and years of pitfalls, or the cold rainy days when it all goes wrong at the track and the long drive home with empty pockets. In fact, had it been one of those days, I have no doubt that Tony would have me down as a mug punter.

Believe me when I tell you that I have had plenty of losing days, but thankfully those days are pretty much behind me now. Whilst it would be wrong to tell you I win all the time, I can tell you with honesty that my betting structure is such that winning and profits are very much a regular pattern with my gambling, providing I adhere to everything myself that I am about to tell you.

I say this because I have been inclined to press on with a winning run and get overconfident, turning a winning day into a losing one. So, I set myself a winning target that I am happy with, and importantly, being careful never to chase my losses. But you have read all of that before and it is nothing new.

As I said, horse racing is not a science, and during the course of this book I will enlighten you with my **Method** and the important way it is implicated, which I guarantee has never been practised before.

It is hard to walk away from a winning streak, but even harder to walk away from a losing one.

The **Method** is unique in the approach to horse racing. It is a niche that I am willing to share with you the reader, especially if you are a punter already. Don't worry if not because I will show you how to work things in your favour, given the right understanding of the sport, and essentially, horse racing is a sport.

I should also point out that my friend Tony would be a particularly good candidate for the pro tipster who sells his information on a subscription basis. Most of whom obtain their customer base, that probably leaked out of a bookmaker's files, or from someone not too honest in the accounts department. How else would I constantly get offered their services when I have never even touched on an enquiry with a tipping service, but I have had lots of accounts with bookmakers over the years (most of them now closed) and my address and phone number has not changed?

Anyway, tipster services are not for me, especially since I met with Stan the Man. I used to see him around the racetracks, and I gave him a lift once during a train strike, and during the journey he told me how he made his money.

Stan would approach a punter at the racetrack who would be queuing to place a bet, usually in the silver ring at a big meeting such as Royal Ascot and with someone looking somewhat affluent, he would pull him to one side and ask him what he was backing.

Whatever the punter told him Stan would dismiss it, telling him to back a certain horse that he was told to back by the trainer or jockey. He would watch whilst the punter had his bet and question him on how much he had on, even asking their name before jotting it all down in his race card. He would then find another mug and do it again with a different horse, and so on, having the top fancied runners covered. He only needed to write down the bookie against each horse and wait for the result and the punter to collect. 'What did I tell you?' Stan would smile, holding his hand out. 'I have got a certainty in the next,' would be his next statement, and on it would go. Who could resist?

I will not be advising you to buy tips from people like Stan. There are, however, some very knowledgeable tipsters in the game who do offer their services selling information, and some are very successful, though finding the right ones can be costly, and not recommended.

BETTING SHOPS

I fully realise the attraction of strolling into a betting shop with a hundred pounds in your pocket and strolling out with three or four hundred. It could very well happen, and sometimes does, but if you are serious about showing a profit for yourself, the betting shop is not the place to be!

The high street betting shops are made welcoming on entry, almost like a private club without membership fees, where you can walk in off the street, have a free coffee and feel part of the establishment without question. Centrally heated and carpeted, with comfy chairs and rest rooms, free newspapers, free pens – all are part of the induction to make you feel important. The staff they employ are generally neutral in their approach, taking your hard-earned cash from you as if you were paying the electricity bill, or buying some groceries, and remember – a bookie has no stock to sell, you are just pitting your wits against theirs, and it's a long way from a level playing field.

But make no mistake, this is an industry like no other. The beehive of precision engineering is working constantly behind the scenes, grinding and grinding 24 hours a day with a regime that is a long way from cast iron, **this is steel!** And those that make the cogs go round are loaded with all kinds of experience in their own individual fields of expertise, such as odds compilers, or those who understand the many facets of the various sporting events. They employ experts with hordes of financial experience, ensuring profits and making sure targets are always met, so when the average punter walks into a betting shop with a few quid in his pocket, the most he has on his side is hope …

Bookmakers are masters at creating confusion, with big screens flashing away every second and high-pitched commentaries on all kinds of sport. They are also keen to spill out helpful tips and pointers to winners because their main objective is turnover; profits will follow automatically…**Theirs**!

How many times have you heard the saying that you never see a poor bookmaker? Which is remarkably true and supports the theory that the punter is at war with them and wants his own pay day, or a little success of their own, and it can and does happen. And nowadays with practically everything visible from satellite or cctv, and you could spot yourself walking into one of those establishments, you would show up like a tiny prick!

Of course, what I mean by that is the fact that whilst over 6,000 licensed betting offices are operating in the UK, one punter analysed alone would be a pin prick against the huge gambling industry. Or it could be the first interpretation is more poignant to them and their way of thinking.

I used to bet with a small bookmaker who happened to be a member of the golf club. Our arrangement was that I could call him and have any bet I liked, and we would settle at the end of the month. He would pay me a cheque, or me him.

I called his private line one morning to call a bet and he told me he was finished. Finally selling to Ladbrokes. He explained that an old lady, who used to have a ten pence each-way accumulator on the dogs every Saturday evening, had five big-priced winners. The bet at the time paid over three thousand pounds. He never saw the old lady until the following Saturday evening as usual, when he paid her the chunk of cash and she then gave him another ten pence each-way accumulator bet, thanked him, and walked out! Not many punters can do that when they have a decent win, especially if standing in the betting shop.

You won't find pro punters or let us say those who make horse racing pay, hanging around in betting shops. If they are not at the races, they will be stuck into the form books at every opportunity, giving them every chance of success, and some do succeed.

It was 1961 before betting shops were allowed to open for business in the UK, with my own experience being deep-rooted in how the punter was treated with disregard, almost contempt. It all goes way back in time to when a board boy, strangely known as a whiteboard man, chalked the runners on a blackboard and waited for the industry feed on how they bet, which came from a Tannoy hanging from a cable somewhere up on the wall. The racing pages of the daily papers, usually the Daily Mirror or the Sun, were cut out and pinned on the walls for the punter to select his fancies, and if he was lucky a copy of the *Sporting Life* might be found in the better establishments – but only some, I hasten to add.

The announcement, such as 'Under orders at Redcar' over the Tannoy, caused panic for those last-minute bets. There were no starting stalls in those days, and whilst the jockeys were getting their positions, punters would be looking over your shoulder, at whatever newspaper was pinned up, hurriedly scribbling out their bets and rushing to the counter before the 'They're off' announcement. Which was followed immediately by the exact time. The punter's bet would always be time clocked stamped; this prevented the clever customer slipping a winning bet across the counter after the race finished.

No pictures of course, he could only listen to the Satellite Information

Service [SIS] commentary that was dreadful at best, generally a crackly feed, supposedly helpful in its introduction, but for whom? … It was commonplace in those days for a race to fall apart at the business end of the commentary giving the description of two runners neck and neck inside a very long last furlong, followed by the call 'Photo Finish.' The anxious wait sometimes resulted in a winning horse, not even mentioned in the last furlong commentary.

If you checked the *Sporting Life* the next day, your own selection, which you told your pals was fighting out the finish, and how unlucky you were, probably faded from the 2-furlong pole. It was as bad as it could be and yet the punters still packed into betting shops in search of that easy money.

SIS was launched initially in 1987 and was broadcast to the licensed betting offices, which unsurprisingly were owned by Ladbrokes, William Hill Organisation, Fred Done, and other bookmakers, all further power to the might that the ordinary Joe punter is up against.

It was some time before the live stream was fed into licensed betting offices (LBOs) and then the competition really began in earnest, with the big boys buying up high street shops and expanding at a rate of knots that had the Monopoly Commission closely monitoring them. Gambling was fast becoming the new thing for the suppressed worker, who for years had been stifled from the source of entertainment that only the privileged were familiar with.

Betting shops were gradually bringing the vision of the wealthy lifestyle of racing folk into the lives of the workforce, which probably upset the upper class who were quite happy doing business with their turf accountant, and yet the independent betting shop owner was still getting a good living with the SIS sound system and scraps of foolscap paper and blunt pencils, that all worked perfectly well for them.

This would obviously falter as the big boys and their fancy duplicate betting slips and comfortable surroundings got bigger, but the ace cards for all those owners of betting shops that held the early LBO licence was territory, along with the government legislation, that only so many licences were issued in any given area. Eventually the offers for the hundreds of independent licences from the big players became too much for the owners of such establishments to refuse, such as my friend from the golf club, which leaves us where we are today with the major operators controlling the betting shop business between them.

It is fair to say that a lot of high street bookmakers' shops are now in serious decline since the betting exchanges took a massive chunk of their trade, but please do not feel in any way sorry for them; they have succeeded in every area of hoovering every last copper from the regular punters' pockets with FOBTs (fixed odds betting terminals) and millions of other ways to lose your money gambling on line, and still do so. But interestingly they can no longer set a price structure for a sporting event of any description as they had done in the past, because they now follow the market that is constructed on each and every betting event by the exchanges such as Betfair, Betdaq and Smarkets, to name just a few.

In many ways this important change which I am highlighting becomes the very aid that helps us, the punter and bettor.

Ironically that market I refer to is constructed by the punter himself, which I will refer to as the **Wisdom of the Crowd.**

It is somewhat of a strange phenomenon which I personally find fascinating, how an invisible force will rule our lives in every aspect.

This force is hugely powerful in everything we try to do and unwittingly we accept its presence without knowing it is there. We go about our regular days doing all the usual things we do – standing in shopping queues, bus, and train queues, road traffic queues, is part of our daily life. Why is it that you always find yourself behind someone? You only ever find yourself in front of the person behind you. What is it that is going on in this strange new world?

I was always familiar and happy with the old one.

I recently tried to see a doctor and was told by a receptionist to call at 8 o'clock the next morning to make an appointment. I called at 2 minutes to 8 and an automated message informed me that I cannot book until 8 o'clock, so I next dialled the number at **exactly** 6 seconds to 8. The automated message then changed, telling me that my call was important to them, asking me to wait and informing me that I was now number 9 in the queue.

We all accept this in some form or another…try booking a decent restaurant, or a holiday or car hire, or getting a gallon of petrol if there is a shortage? Hands up who has ever been first in a queue at an airport to check in. You get there at exactly the time you are informed and find yourself behind two hundred others. I tried beating it once, and I was told the gate is not open yet. I had a quick coffee and was then behind a drove of people who surely fell off the ceiling.

So let us accept this phenomenon and exploit the **wisdom of the crowd** and use its power to our own benefit.

By reading on, I am going to make you happy to sit behind that wisdom!

MUG BETS

I think it is sometimes important to have a gut feeling when gambling. We can get out of bed some mornings and feel lucky, and those feelings can well work. Rushing to buy a lottery ticket because a seagull crapped on you could certainly be described as a mug bet because no logical meaning can be attributed to it.

We should never confuse the art of winning with luck. Winning is about preparation, luck is random.

I have been around some top sportsmen at various times in my life. Footballers, golfers, snooker players; they all possess that same desire to win, which is certainly why they are top sportsmen.

Many years ago, I remember having a cup of tea one morning with Ronnie O'Sullivan's father and asking how he was getting on with his snooker. He told me that young Ronnie was in the snooker room practising, and asked would I care to give him a game for 50 quid with a 20-point start.

Ronnie was 9 years of age at the time and £50 was a big chunk of cash.

Ronnie could not even reach the table without the use of a plastic box to stand on, which he would push around the floor to cue the ball. I used to play a little snooker myself and I have to say I was not bad, so the bet was a steal, or at least I thought so! All I needed was to keep him safe, wait for a mistake and step in. I racked up an early lead with 2 blacks and a blue, and then Ronnie potted a red the length of the table and scored 48 points with ease, and the rest was history, and so was my mug bet.

Happily, no money was exchanged, with big Ron telling me that I never had a prayer, adding that young Ron would be world champion one day.

I thought at the time what a strong statement that was, but somehow, I always believed how possible it was because of his natural talent and total dedication for the game. That snooker game has stuck with me for all these years. Ronnie was then, and still is, a winner!

There is a strong message on why I speak about this because most of us do not possess that power drive to success, and I need you, the reader, to understand the importance of winning and why it matters so much. Try and stand out, and not be the little prick.

We all have a responsibility to manage and control our money without parting with it like some drunken sailor, and having a bet on any sporting event can be exciting and enjoyable. But it is somewhat impossible to explain those feelings to the uninitiated gambler. He just would not understand. Have you ever played a golf game with someone who does not bet? It is like having a Sunday roast without gravy, or a cup of Earl Grey tea with a full English breakfast; it just does not seem right.

Gambling is not how well you bet; it is how well you handle your money.

I have spoken in the foreword about listening to other people's opinions. We all do it, but caution should heed when money is involved, and all that looks gold usually is not.

Arriving back in my office some years ago after a very financially successful Cheltenham meeting, I took a phone call from Tikki, a very close friend of mine, who asked me if I could get a bet on for him?

'Got a tip?' I asked.

'Don't worry about that.' He replied in his usual assertive manner. 'Can you get me a bet on or not?'

'Of course, I can. What is it?'

'I want £400-win trap 2 at Monmore, traps 2&1 £100 forecast and 2&6 £100 forecast. £600 bet.' I took a huge gulp of air and telephoned the bet across. Quite some bet then, and I never had Tikki down for a mug, so I followed him in and doubled the bet. Mel Atreed, a bookmaker I had known for years, took the bet. Mel was fearless when it came to big bets. He had shops and pitches at most racetracks including dog tracks. And our £1,200 bet was everyday money for him. The bet lost and my mug bet for £600 had somewhat undone a decent winning week at Cheltenham.

Tikki was excessive in everything he did, and I should have realised that extended to gambling as well.

On another occasion Tikki arranged for ten of the lads to have a fun day out on Ladies Day at Royal Ascot. We put £200 each in the kitty to cover food and booze and a limousine. We all had a wonderful time. I cannot remember who won or who lost that day, but I do remember calling Tikki the following morning with a suggestion for the £350 that I had left over from the kitty. I suggested three £50 win doubles and a £100 each-way treble on three horses I had selected for the Friday at the Royal Meeting. He overruled me and said, 'Let's have 350 lottery tickets (£1 each at the time). Unbelievably, we never had 3 numbers on any ticket…NOTHING.

The horse bet, incidentally, finished with a 5/1 winner, 6/1 2nd, and 10/1 2nd that would have returned close to £1,100 (quarter odds for most big meetings.)

Lottery and football pools are mug bets in my opinion. They are called pools because of the drips that keep doing them every week but, hey ho, you are buying the dream and for some it has worked.

So - chatting over, it is now time to get to the serious stuff and make some money.

I am not going to tell you which horse wins next year's Derby or give you a cert double for Royal Ascot. That is not going to happen, folks! Besides, that would be a one-off and I would join the vast band of information peddlers who earn their living by tipping horses, and I am certainly not part of that team. Anyway, you would need another book on who to select from the thousands of tipsters out there.

What I will do in this book, however, is steer you towards a way to not only enjoy the sport of kings but give you a massive edge and help you towards very good profits. As you read on you will see that I am keen to bang on about the **Method** because I want to implant this firmly in your mind whenever you place a bet.

I also need you to understand how important the word **Discipline** is, in relation to what you are about to learn. Again, not new information but combined, both words should be foremost in your mind. I want you to use the **Method** to put money in your account or pocket and the **discipline** to keep it just in case you are feeling over-confident and let yourself march on without following what you are about to learn.

First, I must tell you about the guy at the dog track, who was shouting and swearing at the dogs running in each race. A priest standing there listening asked him why he was so violently blaspheming.

He told the priest he had not backed a winner in weeks. The priest told him to follow his example and pray for God's help (yet another invisible force).

So, the man followed what the priest told him, placed his bet on the next race and prayed…

'Please let the six-dog win…Please God, let the six-dog win.'

He looked up and the six-dog led round the first bend; he prayed again.

'Please God, let the six dog win,'…1 lengths clear round the second bend.

He continued his prayer… 'Please God, let the six-dog win'… Looked up and the six dog was ten lengths clear round the last bend. 'Thank you, God, I can take over from here …Come on, you fuckin bastard!'

My reason for telling the dog track gag is something I want you to remember when it is all going your way. Make no mistake, we all want the easy fix with everything in life, but I do not want you to cut corners and drift back into your old gambling ways. Pray to God if it makes you feel any better but keep focussed.

PREPARATION

As mentioned, I play golf, which is a passion I could not live without, but if it meant teeing it up and not having a bet, I would have to say the interest would fade. Even though the bets I strike now on the golf course may well be filed under the last section, mug bets, it would be fair to admit that I do not prepare myself as much as I should, which was never the case some years ago. Whilst everyone was having breakfast, I would be out on the practice field.

Can you imagine the starter rushing in the breakfast room at the British Open, shouting at Rory McIlroy to get on the tee. With him saying, 'I haven't finished my full English yet.'?

Rory would be on the practice field along with every other contestant hours before tee time and usually hours after the day's match. It is a fact of life that preparation is key to success, and even more so when the money is down.

This is now about **you**! And how to get yourself prepared, without cutting corners.

No one mentions the importance of preparation when talking or writing about gambling, but so many punters out there are prepared to go to the dogs or races for a day out with absolutely no preparation at all. The pubs and bars surrounding the tracks on any race meeting are packed with the usual crowds of punters chewing the fat with each other, confidently chatting and joking with each other, and then they walk into the racetrack, wandering around like lost sheep, hoping for that elusive clue.

If you were a carpenter or an electrician you would obviously prepare yourself with the tools of the trade to start earning money, and gambling carries the same principle very much. You will need to get yourself set up with some basic equipment to make your task that much easier.

When I started to get serious about finding winners, I set about getting my own equipment, or shall I say, 'Tools of the trade'? I fully recommend you do similar if you also want to be serious. Do not accept the bookmakers' feed that racing is just fun, it is not! And never was it fun losing money. So never feel comfortable about giving it away.

I realise it is not entirely easy to have your own space where you can bury yourself with your own thoughts. But I have for years now had my own office and television set up, where I can shut myself away and systematically get on with my job of the day. And I recommend for you to do the same if you can.

Any modern-day iPhone carries all the info necessary to hone into any betting site. An iPhone is pretty handy, especially when at the races, but at home a computer is **essential**. Watching the races is also very important, so I have a subscription set up to the Racing Channel on Sky TV. The other racing channel on Sky is free. But most betting sites nowadays have live feeds which enable you to watch races on your computer or iPhone, providing you have set up an account with them, and if you have money in that account, you are able to watch the race live.

The next and **most** important is a monthly subscription to the Racing Post newspaper. I must make it clear at this point that I have absolutely no association with the Racing Post newspaper whatsoever, financial or otherwise, only to point out that the publication is by far the best in the business. In my opinion the contents are invaluable in understanding the racing game and integral to finding the winners with the **Method** that I always use, and which I am close to explaining to you.

You may well be a subscriber to the Racing Post already and have your own way of picking out winners. It might be the tipsters and various pundits' views you find important, most of which can be of use, but who knows what form they might be in on the day, and whose advice are you going for?

Finally, you will need a printer and a couple of packs of paper, and you are just about ready to go.

THE METHOD

And now it is down to the real stuff and the way to make it pay. I will use myself as an example of the route to follow and leave it to you to polish it the way you like it.

Even if I am going to the racetrack I will go through the **Method** religiously every time, which I will refer to throughout the book because this leaves you in no doubt how I need you to think. I really do not want you to drift back into your own ways or become lazy in your administration. It is necessary to understand not only the simplicity of what you are about to read, but the importance of the implication. This is the threshold of gambling that I want you to step into every time you want to bet. The steppingstone to dividends.

On the days I am gambling (which is most days) I usually rise very early and set myself down at my desk with a hot drink and open the Racing Post page on the computer.

I will then click on **Race Cards** that shows all of today's meetings.

Click on any meeting and scroll down to the first race and newspaper form which opens the pdf files. (Only available if you have the subscription.) If newspaper form is not showing, click **pro card**.

When opened the top one says '**card**,' which you download and print (See Image opposite as an example). These sheets are so helpful in their format with just about every important piece of information that is necessary.

THE METHOD

cardsnewmarket (july) 13.07.23

1.50 Bahrain Trophy Stakes (Group 3) (Class 1) £200,000 Total Race Value

ITV 1m 5f

For 3yo **Weights** colts & geldings 9st 3lb, fillies 9st **Penalties** after 2022, a winner of a Group 3 race 3lb; of a Group 1 or Group 2 race 5lb **Penalty value 1st** £113,420 **2nd** £43,000 **3rd** £21,520 **4th** £10,720 **5th** £5,380 **6th** £2,700

GD-FM

Raceform Number	Running Style	Trainer (W-R)	Going (W-R)		Distance	OR	Topspeed	RP Rating		Jockey	

1 (6) 2528 2141-1 **Castle Way** 69 — C Appleby 18% 67-210 8-16 3 9-3 1-2^6w 2-3^119 0-0^3 0-0^0 106 89 89 119 119 William Buick 7-2
2 (5) 3225 12 **Klondike** 68 — W Haggas 73% 24-152 14-47 3 9-3¹ 1-2^60 0-1^115 1-1^90 0-0^0 104 81 81 115 115 Tom Marquand 7-1
3 (2) 4188 0-2127 **Land Legend** 21 — J Ferguson 165% 2-13 1-13 3 9-3 0-1^104 0-1^105 0-0^0 0-0^0 89 88 89 106 106 James Doyle 14-1
4 (3) 4163 5-3112 **Saint George** 22 — A Balding 60% 14-124 9-38 3 9-3 0-0^0 1-2^124 0-0^0 0-0^0 109 110 110 124 124 Cieren Fallon 5-2
5 (4) 4163 6-4599 **Think First** 37 — J Tate 54% 1-19 1-15 3 9-3 0-0^0 0-2^111 0-3^109 0-0^0 95 89 89 110 111 Neil Callan 66-1
6 (1) 4219 15-611 **Tower Of London** 19 D — A P O'Brien IRE 65% 3-30 9-27 3 9-3 0-0^0 3-3^123 0-2^110 1-1^123 109 93 93 123 123 Ryan Moore 6-4

FORM	WINNER	AGE/WT	OR	RPR	DRAW	STALLS	GOING	SP	TRAINER	JOCKEY	HORSE TYPE PREVIOUS BEST

22 42-12 Deauville Legend 3 9-3 — 108^-12 3 of 6 Centre Gd-fm 11-2^4thfav James Ferguson Daniel Muscutt Improver 2nd King George V Handicap (1m4f)
21 11-342 Yibir 3 9-1 — 122³ 3 of 5 Centre Gd-fm 6-4^fav Charlie Appleby James Doyle Exposed 3rd Classic Trial (1m2f)
20 3-51 Al Aasy 3 9-1 — 115^-1 5 of 8 Centre Gd-sft 3-1^2ndfav William Haggas Jim Crowley Improver won NmkII (1m4f)
19 31-52 Spanish Mission 3 9-1 — 121^-3 1 of 9 High Gd-fm 13-2^4thfav David Simcock Jamie Spencer Improver 2nd Gdwd List (1m3f)
18 11-66 Wells Farhh Go 3 9-1 — 123^9 4 of 8 Centre Gd-fm 7-1^4thfav Tim Easterby David Allan Improver 6th King Edward VII (1m4f)

FATE OF FAVOURITES: 5210050214
TRAINERS IN THIS RACE (w-pl-r): A P O'Brien 1-2-6,Charlie Appleby 1-1-5,James Ferguson 1-0-1,William Haggas 1-0-3,Andrew Balding 0-1-5

2.25 Kingdom Of Bahrain July Stakes (Group 2) (Colts & Geldings) (Class 1) £100,000 Total Race Value ITV 6f

For 2yo colts & geldings **Weights** 9st 2lb **Penalties** a winner of a Group 1 or Group 2 race 3lb **Penalty value 1st** £56,710 **2nd** £21,500 **3rd** £10,760 **4th** £5,360 **5th** £2,690 **6th** £1,350

GD-FM

1 (3) 3338 1 **Chief Mankato** 65 D — C Hills 67% 10-80 4-26 2 9-2 1-1^101 0-0^0 0-0^0 1-1^101 — 90 90 101 101 William Buick 11-2
2 (1) 3535 21 **Jasour** 39 — Clive Cox 52% 7-45 4-26 2 9-2 1-1^94 0-1^92 0-0^0 0-0^0 — 65 85 94 94 Jim Crowley 16-1
3 (7) 3898 1 **Lake Forest** 29 D — W Haggas 73% 24-152 14-47 2 9-2 1-1^100 0-0^0 0-0^0 1-1^100 — 52 52 100 100 Tom Marquand 7-1
4 (8) 4187 12 **Male** 21 — R Fahey 40% 3-63 9-57 2 9-2 1-2^115 0-0^0 0-0^0 0-0^0 104 104 104 115 115 Oisin Orr 7-2
5 (2) 4164 110 **Maximum Impact** 22 — A Haynes 58% 0-7 3-34 2 9-2 0-1^0 1-1^101 1-1^101 0-0^0 93 — 97 — 105 David Egan 16-1
6 (6) 4601 61 **Mountain Bear** 13 D — A P O'Brien IRE 65% 3-30 9-27 2 9-2 0-0^0 1-2^105 0-0^0 1-2^105 — 78 78 105 105 Ryan Moore 4-1
7 (9) 3937 1 **Purosangue** 28 — A Balding 60% 14-124 9-38 2 9-2 1-1^101 0-0^0 0-0^0 0-0^0 — 91 91 101 101 Ray Dawson 5-2
8 (4) 4187 1 **Thunder Blue** 21 D — D Ffrench Davis 33% 1-3 0-9 2 9-2 1-3^105 0-0^0 0-0^0 1-2^104 94 93 96 105 105 Sean Levey 14-1
9 (5) 4187 310 **Toca Madeira** 21 — B Meehan 71% 4-66 0-4 2 9-2 1-3^98 0-0^0 0-0^0 1-1^98 84 73 77 87 98 Sean Levey 40-1

FORM	WINNER	AGE/WT	OR	RPR	DRAW	STALLS	GOING	SP	TRAINER	JOCKEY	HORSE TYPE PREVIOUS BEST

22 112 Persian Force 2 9-2 — 118⁰ 3 of 7 Centre Gd-fm 2-1^fav Richard Hannon Rossa Ryan Improver 2nd Coventry (6f)
21 131 Lusail 2 9-0 — 109^-10 7 of 10 Centre Gd-fm 15-2^4thfav Richard Hannon Pat Dobbs Improver won NmkJ (7f)
20 31 Tactical 2 9-0 — 115^-1 6 of 10 High Gd-sft 5-2^2ndfav Andrew Balding William Buick Improver won Windsor Castle (5f)
19 17 Royal Lytham 2 9-0 — 113⁰ 8 of 8 High Gd-fm 11-1^4thfav A P O'Brien Wayne Lordan Improver 7th Coventry (6f)
18 12 Advertise 2 9-0 — 126⁰ 6 of 8 High Gd-fm 10-1^0fav Martyn Meade Frankie Dettori In form 2nd Coventry (6f)

FATE OF FAVOURITES: 4121413451
TRAINERS IN THIS RACE (w-pl-r): A P O'Brien 1-2-9,Andrew Balding 1-0-2,Brian Meehan 0-1-4,Charles Hills 0-0-2,Clive Cox 0-1-2,Richard Fahey 0-2-5,William Haggas 0-1-2

3.00 bet365 Handicap (Heritage Handicap) (Class 2) £100,000 Total Race Value ITV 6f

For 3yo Rated 0-105 **Weights** highest weight not less than 9st 9lb **Minimum weight** 8-2 **Penalties** after June 24th, each race won 6lb **Penalty value 1st** £51,540 **2nd** £24,170 **3rd** £12,090 **4th** £6,040 **5th** £3,020 **6th** £1,510

GD-FM

1 (3) 4131 211126 **Desert Cop** 23 D — A Balding 60% 14-124 9-38 3 9-9 0-0^0 0-3^112 0-0^0 2-4^112 105 83 94 110 117 Harry Davies (3) 12-1
2 (13) 1144 213-27 **Alpha Capture** 131 D — W Haggas 73% 24-152 14-47 3 9-6 0-1^92 1-1^95 1-2^114 2-5^114 100 99 101 93 114 Tom Marquand 16-1
3 (9) 4046 124-63 **Mill Stream** 26 D — Jane Chapple-Hyam 36% 12-75 1-6 3 9-3 1-4^117 0-1^107 0-0^0 1-4^117 99 98 98 117 117 Marco Ghiani 10-1
4 (16) 4038 1-12 **Tajalla** 26 — R Varian 78% 18-130 7-35 3 9-1 0-1^115 1-1^107 0-1^113 0-0^0 97 92 92 115 115 David Egan 10-1
5 (12) 4046 9-0222 **Washington Heights** 28 BF — K A Ryan 40% 6-51 7-28 3 8-12 1-2^111 0-3^114 0-3^110 0-1^118 94 100 100 118 118 Ryan Moore 5-1
6 (15) 4046 4-0570 **Rousing Encore** 90 D — R Fahey 40% 3-63 9-57 3 8-12 1-4^111 1-4^110 0-3^99 1-8^116 94 59 77 86 116 Oisin Orr 20-1
7 (4) 4191 742140 **Dark Thirty** 21 D — R Hannon 16% 42-321 10-56 3 8-9 0-5^113 2-3^116 0-3^113 1-1^111 91 57 90 98 116 Sean Levey 33-1
8 (11) 4046 611111 **Quinault** 26 D — S C Williams 38% 11-132 0-18 3 8-8n 2-3^110 2-2^115 0-0^0 4-4^119 90 100 100 120 120 Connor Planas (5) 7-1
9 (17) 4229 9-7516 **Frankness** 20 D — A Balding 60% 14-124 9-38 3 8-8 1-3^121 1-2^110 1-4^103 1-3^121 90 80 80 105 121 Callum Hutchinson (3) 11-2
10 (5) 4046 3-4334 **Eminency** 26 — Clive Cox 52% 7-45 4-26 3 8-6 0-1^116 0-1^116 0-2^110 1-6^117 88 97 102 117 117 John Fahy 10-1
11 (6) 4627 4-6532 **Animate** 12 — S & E Crisford 72% 5-42 5-30 3 8-5p 0-0^0 0-3^109 0-0^0 0-1^0 87^-3 75 88 120 120 Andrea Atzeni 12-1
12 (8) 4046 90-036 **Redemption Time** 26 — Clive Cox 52% 7-45 4-26 3 8-5h 1-4^116 0-3^109 0-1^75 0-2^115 87 95 95 116 116 Ray Dawson 20-1
13 (10) 3587 231-1 **Tough Enough** 36 D — J Tate 54% 1-19 1-15 3 8-5h 1-1^117 0-1^104 0-1^101 2-4^117 87 92 104 117 117 Hayley Turner 10-1
14 (7) 4647 26315 **Ferrous** 12 BF — J Channon 67% 2-0 4-16 3 8-4 1-2^115 0-1^91 1-3^106 1-4^116 86 95 108 106 115 Aidan Keeley (3) 22-1
15 (1) 4229 79-700 **Brave Nation** 20 — Michael Bell 41% 5-96 0-19 3 8-3 1-5^116 0-1^95 0-1^104 0-3^104 85 63 76 92 109 J F Egan 66-1
16 (14) 4229 7152-5 **Executive Decision** 26 — J Osborne 42% 0-21 3-18 3 8-3h 0-1^109 0-2^99 1-1^111 1-3^111 85 84 104 105 113 Saffie Osborne 20-1
17 (2) 4118 65-11 **Be Frank** 26 D — H Candy 40% 7-43 1-5 3 8-2 1-2^109 1-2^113 0-1^98 2-4^119 84 92 92 119 119 George Rooke 10-1

FORM	WINNER	AGE/WT	OR	RPR	DRAW	STALLS	GOING	SP	TRAINER	JOCKEY	HORSE TYPE PREVIOUS BEST

22 314142 Lethal Levi 3 8-3 85 114^-1 14 of 19 Centre Gd-fm 16-1^8thfav K R Burke Jimmy Quinn Improver won Yarm Hcap (6f)
21 217-72 Blackrod 3 8-6 87 115^-2 16 of 19 Centre Gd-fm 11-1^9thfav Michael Dods Silvestre De Sousa Improver 2nd Pavers Sprint Handicap (6f)
20 0311- Elon 3 8-6 87 110^-6 12 of 20 High Soft 40-1^13thfav William Knight Callum Shepherd Improver Seasonal Debutant
18 3-371 Pass The Vino 3 8-4 85 110^-3 20 of 20 High Gd-fm 25-1^13thfav Paul D'Arcy David Egan Improver won Wolv Auct (6f)
18 -22111 Foxtrot Lady 3 8-12 94 116^-3 8 of 20 High Gd-fm 8-1^8thfav Andrew Balding David Probert Improver won Carl Hcap (6f)

FATE OF FAVOURITES: 2346000303
TRAINERS IN THIS RACE (w-pl-r): Andrew Balding 2-0-4,Richard Fahey 1-3-15,Roger Varian 1-0-4,Clive Cox 0-2-3,Henry Candy 0-1-2,Kevin Ryan 0-2-11,Richard Hannon 0-3-12,William Haggas 0-3-7

Image 001. A visual of a typical Racing Post pdf sheet.

These files are referred to throughout the book, and can be essential in final decision making.

35

Firstly, I want to draw your attention to the column furthest right on the pdf called the **Tissue.** In betting terms, a **tissue** price is the odds that all newspapers print underneath every race. This will become both important and fundamental to the **Method,** and I want you to fully understand why, even if you are very familiar with horse racing and gambling, and more so if not.

Tissue prices are only a guide which is made up for every horse race in every racing paper. The odds compilers, whose job it is to do them, construct one of the most difficult and important parts of the gambling system. For a start, they need a very good understanding of form and handicapping to publish those prices every day. These prices will give you a guide, for every runner, on how the betting may or should open up, but remember they will vary from paper to paper, which is the reason I use the Racing Post, who employ the best odds compilers in the business, and it is **always** those tissue prices I work from. Never do I mix them up with other newspapers.

I write those exact prices alongside every runner on the racing page of my newspaper including the prices for **Non-runners** (See Image 002 opposite as an example).

I then click on 'select bookmaker' above the Racing Post card and select one of the bookmaker's odds. This shows, at a touch, the best price currently on offer from for every individual horse.

Importantly, I then write down those prices to the right of the tissue prices that I have written down already.

If I do not have a Racing Post for whatever reason and I am only working with the pdf file, which is ok, I will write the current odds by the side of the printed tissue prices on the pdf.

Now I become aware of the importance about including the non-runners in the prices, and I urge you to do the same and not skip any of this process.

Image 002. Example of early Racing Post tissue prices and post-time odds to the right and any non runners.

Also we create our own outsiders, the tissued 33/1 shot ran 3rd.

By doing it this way you will also clearly see the different price structure of the new market. In other words, how much the price structure of the race has altered because of the non-runners.

Rather than confuse anyone with betting percentages here, I have covered this on page pages 83 and 84 for those wishing to be more technical.

Any non-runner will obviously reflect on the other runners' prices, and this is important. For example, and to help you understand the importance of non-runners, let me draw your attention to a horse that is unruly at the start and is withdrawn.

A Rule 4 applies, and a percentage is taken from winning

bets depending on the price of the withdrawn horse at the time, because the market has not had time to reconstruct. In other words, without it running in the race, the other horses would be reduced in price, so if a horse is priced at, let's say, 9/4 in the **original** tissue and is trading at say 5/2 with a 5/1 non-runner out of the reckoning, there is a very strong indication that this runner is not fancied at all, although its price still looks as though it is reflecting its chance.

I am creating my own method of assessment with very little effort here, and it is now that I work on my **Elimination** process.

In other words, I cross out the ones that have extended in price. **A very important part of the process.**

This does not mean a 6/1 shot showing at 13/2 or 7/1 should be written off! These horses should still be treated as **live** runners. It does mean; however, the bookies are slightly generous with the odds of this horse, which says 'Caution!' because they are **never** generous. I may well leave this one perhaps with a question mark, but I will, however, put a line through, let's say, a 14/1 shot trading at 20s or a 25/1 price now showing at 33s, or most importantly a 6/4 favourite trading at 5/2 creates a massive negative with me, and it is these changes in the market that interest me most because the big picture is beginning to unfold, always remember in your mind, the many thousands of hardened form experts (**wisdom of the crowd**) are working for you.

This is now becoming your edge on the bookmaker. You are effectively turning a 15-runner race into a 3- or 4-runner race.

I can remember standing at the dog tracks where everyone is looking for clues. Time after time the bookie's runner shouts at the board man, '**No six dog, Harry**!' normally as the dogs are going in the traps, and the punters knock his stand over trying to get the price that was showing. They all manage to get on strangely, and the six dog is still running.

Confusion, as I said earlier, is a big tool for the bookmaker, because loads of people who gamble, and go racing, really don't know what it is all about, or most importantly who is going to win. This includes the bookmaker, who only wants to put money in his satchel in line with the overround (See page 83 and 84).

The picture is now becoming very real in information terms, and we are getting our own edge because we have now established a definite weakness in the market and, more importantly, a strength, and as the clock nears to post time it often becomes even more visible.

Look again at the visual. You can see by doing this, a 17-runner race is reduced to a much easier to solve 8-runner race. This is only your starting point. Do not rush with your decision, pace it through as much as you can and follow the above with confidence before you bet. Put the information in place. If you cannot choose between 2 runners, for example, split your stake, back them both, or if it becomes too buzzy, simply do not bet.

Also, as you can see from the visual, we are not simply crossing off the outsiders, as some might suggest, we are making different outsiders. Number 7 was the biggest tissue outsider originally, that now becomes a visibly different betting proposition, and one of the eight runners.

I want you to remember this is not a science, and horses are not steam engines that run in straight lines on rails. Quite often a horse drifts in the market and wins. So, understanding the drifts and market moves is essentially the reason I spell the **Method** out, because overall it works and creates very good profits.

You may well be thinking by now that you know this. A horse is being backed and you can follow the market. That mindset is **not** where I am going with this, I am putting you in control and steering you away from the regular pattern of horse racing that has been in place for more years than I care to remember. This is the shovel I spoke of.

Firstly, a single non-runner at 66/1 here would not be significant enough to reduce the odds of the other runners and on checking the result for this event, the winner just happened to suit the **Method.** (I swear not selected by choice.)

Quinault	Tissued 7/1	Won 4/1
Mill Stream	Tissued 10/1	2nd 7/1
Dark Thirty	Tissued 33/1	3rd 20/1

One of my pet hates when watching a race on TV is the presenter announcing that a particular horse has been backed, highlighting what looks like a lot of money for it. To give you an example which happened on the opening day of the flat 2022 at Kempton Park in the 3.55 race: a horse called Papa Stour was running in an 8-runner race. The tissue I had written down earlier that morning in my Racing Post said 10/1. The right handwritten best odds price was 12/1. So, in an 8-runner race Papa Stour was not really a live runner, and good reason to cross it off. During the morning that early price drifted out to 16/1, solid reason now to dismiss it and cross it off. As the horses were parading, there was a show of 14/1 for Papa Stour. Then we were shown a visual, highlighted on the TV screen, clearly showing 18/1, 16/1, 14/1, which on the face of it, and if I did not know better, was looking like a pretty serious gamble was happening.

My **Method** exposes that... **no gamble at all** was taking place. It was likely that punters were seeing that horse trading at 18/1, which was looking like value compared to the 10/1 in their paper, and the price was too big, or they were following the money on what looks like a gamble. Even at that point Papa Stour was trading **4 points above the tissue.** This is the important stuff here that I need to drum into your betting stride. The horse went out at the off to 18s again, it was unplaced.

In fact, the **Method** shone like a beacon on that race and won me a very big chunk of dosh.

The 2/1 favourite, Royal Crusade, was uneasy at around 5/2, so it quickly became a definite race of interest for me. The second favourite, Tommy De Vito, tissue 3/1, was trading at 9/2, and the third favourite Ejtilaab, tissued at 11/2, was trading at 3s. The other tissued 11/2 shot Whittle Le Woods, also trading much shorter than the tissue price at 7/2. The other 4 runners traded accordingly

Rathbone	R/P Tissue	10/1 trading at 16/1
Papa Stour	R/P Tissue	10/1 trading 18/1
The Last Lion	R/P Tissue	12/1 trading at 25/1
Repartee	R/P Tissue	25/1 traded at 40/1

So, what we had here was an 8-runner race reduced to 2.

Whittle Le Woods and Ejtilaab.

(See Image 003, overleaf) My decision to bet was based on the weakness of the front two in the market, together with the back four who were so overpriced the bookies could not give them away. So, with a little research on them both I opened the wallet.

It was a no-brainer. Whittle Le Woods had won 4 of his last 7 races and clearly had a very busy season already, but his last winning mark of 83 with a 3lb claimer meant that he was 6lb higher today and 6lb more than he had ever been, whereas Ejtilaab had been competing in listed and group races, and given 2lb by the handicapper from his last run.

Ejtilaab won easily by two and a half lengths.

I pointed out earlier that you may well want to polish up your own decisions when placing a bet, which brings me back to the importance of the pdf files where you can see quickly relevant information that will help you in making your final decision to bet …trainer form, ground preference, speed figures, etc,

41

Image 003. All pointers were showing Papa Stour being backed. HE WAS NOT! Check your own odds to determine what is being backed.

3.55 RACE 5

Try Our New Price Boosts At Unibet Handicap (London Sprint Series Qualifier) (Class 2)

RTV

Winner £12,885

6f AW

£25,000 Total Race Value **For** 4yo+ Rated 86-105 (also open to such horses rated 106 and 107; such horses rated 85 and below are also eligible - see Standard Conditions) **Weights** highest weight 9st 7lb **Minimum Weight** 8-2 **Penalties** after March 19th, each race won, 4-6yo 5lb; 7yo+ 4lb **Royal Crusade's Handicap Mark** 105 **Entries** 13 pay £125 **Penalty value 1st** £12,885 **2nd** £6,042.50 **3rd** £3,022.50 **4th** £1,510 **5th** £755 **6th** £377.50 DRAW ADVANTAGE: SLIGHT MIDDLE

1 (7)	75731-2 **ROYAL CRUSADE** 71 **BF D1 Ply1** CD1 *b g Shamardal-Zibelina* **Charlie Appleby** Godolphin	p5 9-7 ¹Jack Mitchell	(118)
2 (3)	1P3-553 **EJTILAAB** (IRE) 21 **D3 Ply1** *b g Slade Power-Miranda Frost* **Charlie Fellowes** Paul Wildes	6 9-7 Callum Shepherd	(116)
3 (4)	21/03-4 **THE LAST LION** (IRE) 83 **D1 Ply1** CD1 *b g Choisir-Mala Mala* **Charlie & Mark Johnston** John Brown, Megan Dennis & Partner	8 8-13 Joe Fanning	(116)
4 (8)	135/1-1 **TOMMY DE VITO** 58 **D2 Ply1** CD1 *b g Dandy Man-Rohlindi* **Charles Hills** Chelsea Thoroughbreds - Goodfellas	5 8-6 ¹Luke Morris	(119)
5 (1)	29008-4 **RATHBONE** 44 **BF D4** *b g Foxwedge-Frequent* **Kevin Ryan** Mrs Angie Bailey	6 8-6 Megan Nicholls	(115)
6 (5)	/5708-5 **REPARTEE** (IRE) 23 **D2** *br g Invincible Spirit-Pleasantry* **Tony Carroll**² R Barney	5 8-6 ¹Hayley Turner	(115)
7 (6)	452-113 **PAPA STOUR** (USA) 14 **D1 Ply5** C2 CD1 *b g Scat Daddy-Miaundgiass* **Stuart Williams** T W Morley	tp7 8-4 Lorenzo Atzori(7)	(117)
8 (2)	1214211 **WHITTLE LE WOODS** 14 **D4 Ply1** *b g Lethal Force-Lady Loch* **Michael Appleby** The Horse Watchers 4	p4 8-2 ¹Thore Hammer Hansen	(118)

2021 (7 ran) **Great Ambassador** (2) Ed Walker 4 8-8 9/4   Luke Morris OR90

BETTING FORECAST: 2 Royal Crusade, 3 Tommy de Vito, 11-2 Ejtilaab, Whittle Le Woods, 10 Papa Stour, Rathbone, 12 The Last Lion, 25 Repartee.

or maybe you have your own process of evaluation, but the above information, exactly the way that I have spelt it out, should always be the overriding factor or, should I say, the starting point for all decisions made.

Let me at this point dissect the word **Value** in relation to racing.

Essentially when gambling, we are dealing with odds, and how they are displayed. This is what we are betting on, getting more, or getting less for our money. Clever marketing will have you believe that what is being offered is the best value on offer and the cheapest, and bookmakers try and hammer home that very philosophy. How foolish do you feel paying a certain price for something and your neighbour tells you he or she bought it for so much cheaper? Purplebricks and McDonald's are constantly pumping that very concept, which is exactly how bookmakers work, and that is where most people will get it wrong, ending up with empty trouser pockets

Value is on everyone's mind with most things in life, but when it comes to gambling it is never more important, as so many pundits will have you believe. Or is it?

Remember all those books out there on the subject, that we should by now get tired of reading. Obviously 6/1 is better than 5/1, but for me it shows much more.

Firstly, **why** is 6/1 being offered for a horse that has been trading at 5/1? If you dismiss the fact that the bookmaker is being generous there are two reasons.

One, the bookmaker has larger investments on other horses in that race, and needs to level his book, or two, he is testing the market to find any serious interest. Remember, he does not know what is going to win the race. He himself is following the market just as you are, and whilst you are looking at his board, his bookkeeper behind him is carefully watching the fast-changing market on his computer feed to the betting exchange and relaying the prices to the man up front.

So, if you go steaming in to a 5/1 shot that he has just marked up at 6/1, it will be at least 13/2 or 7/1 on the exchange or probably bigger. If it transpires that the interest at 6/1 is too much, the bookmaker will go back to 5/1 on his board and generally fall in line with everyone else, and at the track I will guarantee this uncertainty in every race.

But always remember this is what I speak about when watching and getting the important feel for the market when you are at the track. You are getting your own very clear feed with the written facts of the race in your newspaper. Seeing a horse slashed from 7/1 to 5/1 and diving in is something I never do, that will only compromise the **Method**. I watch calmly what is happening with the **Method** before stepping in, if at all. The **Method** is my market, and sometimes I get it wrong myself, but these are my guns that I always stick to.

Also, the word **discipline** is very important here, and we should all learn when to refuse a bet and sit on our hands.

The three-day Craven meeting at Newmarket in April is always an informative meeting on the flat because it can highlight some of the early form and give an idea of what stables are trying. I never fancied the Tuesday card 2022 for betting purposes, but there was a massive move on the **Method**, in the first race, where I should not have played, and it cost me a nice few quid steaming into a horse that was a big early morning buzz. If you, the reader, had been sitting in my class, I would have rapped your knuckles with the ruler for being so stupid and pointed out the silly mistake (see image 004).

Firstly, a ten-runner 5-furlong maiden fillies' stakes, for un-raced 2-year-olds, is a watching brief and **not** a betting race, and the bookmakers are the ones who have had their fingers burnt many times with solid gambles and they will always over-egg the pudding in terms of value. In other words, they show a bigger degree of caution in the run-up to post time with this type of race if anything is shown to be backed early.

Secondly, with un-raced horses the whispers from the gallops turn into shouts, owners turn into tipsters and, hey presto, a gamble is beginning to gather pace. And why would the bookie want to pay out on a 12/1 shot if they can reduce the price and make it a 4/1 shot? Of course, by doing so it pushes the other runners' prices out.

In the early years, the bookmakers offered guaranteed prices during the mornings, in their crafty quest to get the feel for the market under the proviso that they were being generous. The truth is that you could only get peanuts on and, importantly for them, this information of horses wanted to be backed would be fed back to head office and then fed to the track for opening shows fifteen minutes before post time, and if you had any doubt about how important this all is, consider that crucial edge being theirs, and not yours. Plus, the added fact this only applied to handicaps, and never on 2-and 3-year-old maiden races.

But now the early prices with all races on tomorrow's racing are being mopped up on the Betting Exchanges whilst you are cleaning your teeth before you go to bed, and the bookies can do nothing about it only to reflect those prices in the early shows, and what looks like a big gamble is over exaggerated, so be careful not to be suckered in.

In fact, you can even see for yourself the actual amount gambled early on most exchange sites, and generally it is quite small, because the market is slowly and gradually being tested, and very little is ever being offered early doors. Another point worth remembering here, speaking about gambles, is the fact that syndicate runners and the like, whose members know little about racing and betting, can often affect or create a false gamble simply by spreading the word, and the syndicate horse gambles will often fall flat.

However, it makes perfect sense if there is a very strong buzz for a single horse, and those who do know about it would obviously want to get the best price they can and get on early. Which clearly supports the **Method**. Though, if two or three horses are fancied in the same race, this creates confusion in the market which you need to understand before you make your decision to bet, or to sit on your hands.

The Newmarket race (Image 004 opposite) unfolded as follows...

Lost Angel was tissued at 3/1 in the R/P and was showing early at 7/1 (a price that must have thrilled the many value seekers.)

Second in was Bojink tissued at 7/2 showing 9/2 early.

Flying Barty tissued at 9/2 was showing at 11/2.

Powerdress and Yahsat were both tissued at 7/1 and both steady all morning, which I always refer to as live runners.

Dreaming Princess was tissued 8/1 and showing 11/1 early.

Radio Goo Goo 8/1 and 11/2 early.

Family Ties 12/1 and 4/1 early, looked a massive move, but was still trading as a 4/1 favourite in a 10-runner race, subsequently drifting out to 5/1.

Lucy Lightfoot was 25/1 and 20/1.

Cloud Flyer was 33/1 and 40/1.

Powerdress and Yahsat had the race between them at the finish with Powerdress coming out on top, with a starting price of 8/1.

When a race begins to develop a pattern like this, for me it is obvious and very clear that nothing, apart from confusion, is happening.

The truth is, at the off, two horses traded at 9/2 joint favourite (5/1 each in places). The bookies are almost screaming at you, **'Look how generous we are! How much more can we help you?'**

Interestingly, the two horses that fought out the finish actually supported the **Method**, in as much as their prices **had** to be pushed out because of the big move on Family Ties, but they were always live runners, though primarily it was a no-betting race.

The bookies were not so generous on the second day, Fillies Maiden at Newmarket with the Roger Varian runner who had proven form. Tissued at 6/4, never better than evens early, and bolted up by nearly 4 lengths.

1.15 **bet365 British EBF Maiden Fillies' Stakes (GBB Race) (Class 4)** ITV4
RACE 1 Winner £5,400 — 5f Row

£10,000 Total Race Value **For** 2yo fillies which are EBF eligible **Weights** 9st **Entries** 18 pay £50 **Penalty value**
1st £5,400 2nd £2,535 3rd £1,268 4th £634 DRAW ADVANTAGE: SLIGHT LOW
ADJUSTED AVERAGE WINNING RPR 96

1 (3) **BOJINK** (IRE) — ch f Galileo Gold-Tanbo — William Buick — 2 9-0
George Boughey Nick Bradley Racing 44

2 (9) **CLOUD FLYER** — b f Fastnet Rock-Wittgenstein — Dayverson de Barros — 2 9-0
George Boughey O Oulton

3 (7) **DREAMING PRINCESS** — b f Oasis Dream-Lisiere — Rossa Ryan — 2 9-0
David Loughnane Amo Racing Limited

4 (8) **FAMILY TIES** (IRE) — b f Expert Eye-Savannah's Dream — Daniel Tudhope — 2 9-0
David O'Meara Clipper Logistics

5 (6) **FLYING BARTY** (IRE) — b f Starspangledbanner-Dice Game — Kevin Stott — 2 9-0
Kevin Ryan Chasemore Farm & Seymour Bloodstock

6 (2) **LOST ANGEL** (IRE) — gr f Dark Angel-Last Bid — Liam Keniry — 2 9-0
Clive Cox Atlantic Equine

7 (4) **LUCY LIGHTFOOT** (IRE) — b f Fast Company-Redoutable — Marco Ghiani — 2 9-0
Stuart Williams J W Parry And Mrs C Shekells

8 (10) **POWERDRESS** (IRE) — b f Dandy Man-Nuclear Option — Sean Levey — 2 9-0
Richard Hannon Martin Hughes

9 (5) **RADIO GOO GOO** — b f Havana Grey-Radio Gaga — James Doyle — 2 9-0
David Evans Brian Mould, Richard Kent & Partner

10 (1) **YAHSAT** (IRE) — b f Dandy Man-Barqeyya — Clifford Lee — 2 9-0
K R Burke Saeed Bin Mohammed Al Qassimi

2021 (12 ran) Desert Dreamer (6) Stuart Williams 2 9-0 25/1 — Hollie Doyle RPR78

BETTING FORECAST: 3 Lost Angel, **7-2** Bojink, **9-2** Flying Barty, **7** Powerdress, Yahsat, **8** Dreaming Princess, Radio Goo Goo, **12** Family Ties, **25** Lucy Lightfoot, **33** Cloud Flyer.

Image 004.

Unraced 2 year olds are not a betting proposition.

Check the betting pattern that I have spelt out.

Not the time to take on those generous bookmakers.

Also, a second **Method** runner won that afternoon at 7/2 that more than covered Tuesday's bad wager. I had some business planned the next day, and never went to Newmarket. Had I done so, and just betting blind on the **Method,** I could have backed six winners. Namely…

Out From Under	Tissued 2/1	Won at 8/11
Tajalla	Tissued 2/1	Won at 11/8
Tuscan	Tissued 9/1	Won at 11/2
Coase	Tissued 10/1	Won at 9/2
Accidental Agent	Tissued 9/1	Won at 13/2
Twilight Falls	Tissued 3/1	Won at 6/5

Not that I suggest you bet blind on the **Method**. I would always hope that you would dot a few i's and cross a few t's. I am merely pointing out just how powerful it is, even without the hours of study – it can, and often will, bring results!

OK, let us summarise the facts laid out in the **Method** in the simplest of terms, and to make it easy and completely understandable.

I have chosen a horse race at the very highest level - the Epsom Derby 2021 - with a field of 12 runners going to post (see Image 005 & 006 opposite).

Sorry if I might bang on about this one, but it was a very memorable day for me and I won an awful lot of money on that particular card, and perhaps had a big say in bringing this book together.

For the purpose of those at the back not paying much attention I will assume everyone is going to have a bet, that is risk your money on one horse that will hopefully win. Or alternatively eliminate 11 horses that are going to lose.

Never lose sight of this instruction because eliminating horses is the very essence of the **Method** that shows us clearly the importance of crossing them off, and what you are left with. Your task is made that bit easier on both counts on this occasion because there is a non-runner.

For this scenario, let us say you arranged a game of golf for that morning, or promised to take the wife out shopping. But before you did anything, and even though the tissue prices are all typed underneath in the betting forecast, you

4.30 Cazoo Derby

RACE 5 (Class 1, Group 1)

Winner £637,987.50

ITV

(1m4f6y) **1M4f**

£1,125,000 guaranteed **For** 3yo colts & fillies **Weights** colts 9st; fillies 8st 11lb
First entries 389 pay £420 **First forfeit** 116 pay £825 **2nd entries** 7 pay £6,750
Second forfeit 23 pay £2550 **Confirmations** 19 pay £2,100
Penalty value 1st £637,987.50 **2nd** £241,875.00 **3rd** £121,050.00
4th £60,300.00 **5th** £30,262.50 **6th** £15,187.50

41-22	**ADAYAR (IRE)** ITF 28 BF S1		3 9-0
1 (1)	b c Frankel-Anna Salai		¹Adam Kirby (122)
	Charlie Appleby Godolphin		
315-11	**BOLSHOI BALLET** (IRE) ITF 27 S1		3 9-0
2 (9)	b c Galileo-Alla Anna		Ryan Moore (131)
	A P O'Brien (IRE) Magnier/Tabor/Smith/Westerberg		
1141-5	**GEAR UP** (IRE) ITF 23 S1		3 9-0
3 (6)	b c Teofilo-Gearanai		Ben Curtis (124)
	Mark Johnston Teme Valley		
1-11	**HURRICANE LANE** (IRE) ITF 23 S1		3 9-0
4 (5)	ch c Frankel-Gale Force		William Buick (128)
	Charlie Appleby Godolphin		
4-11	**JOHN LEEPER** (IRE) ¹⁰		3 9-0
5 (12)	b c Frankel-Snow Fairy		¹Frankie Dettori (121)
	Ed Dunlop Anamoine Limited		
9181-41	**MAC SWINEY** (IRE) ITF 14 S4		3 9-0
6 (8)	ch c New Approach-Halfway to Heaven		Kevin Manning (133)
	J S Bolger Mrs J S Bolger		
72 11-1	**MOHAAFETH** (IRE) 35 S1		3 9-0
7 (4)	ch c Frankel-French Dressing		Jim Crowley (131)
	William Haggas Shadwell Estate Company Ltd		
2-2	**MOJO STAR** (IRE) 22 BF		3 9-0
8 (10)	b c Sea The Stars-Gallery		¹David Egan (111)
	Richard Hannon Amo Racing Limited		
21312-6	**ONE RULER** (IRE) 35 S1		3 9-0
9 (11)	b c Dubawi-Fintry		James Doyle (127)
	Charlie Appleby Godolphin		
2-16	**SOUTHERN LIGHTS** (IRE) 27		3 9-0
10 (3)	b c Sea The Stars-Owenna		Declan McDonogh (116)
	Joseph Patrick O'Brien (IRE) Aquis Racing & Al Mamoura P'ship		
5-11	**THIRD REALM** (IRE) ITF		3 9-0
11 (2)	b c Sea The Stars-Reem Three		Andrea Atzeni (125)
	Roger Varian Sheikh Mohammed Obaid Al Maktoum		
413-41	**YOUTH SPIRIT** (IRE) ITF 31 D1 S2		3 9-0
12 (7)	b c Kodiac-Rocana		Tom Marquand (124)
	Andrew Balding Ahmad Al Shaikh		

2020 (16 ran) Serpentine (12) A P O'Brien 3 9-0 25/1   Emmet McNamara RPR121

BETTING FORECAST: 13-8 Bolshoi Ballet, 11-2 Mac Swiney, 7 Hurricane Lane, Mohaafeth, 8 John Leeper, 12 Third Realm, 22 Gear Up, One Ruler, 25 Southern Lights, 28 Youth Spirit, 33 Adayar, 100 Mojo Star.

4.30 Cazoo Derby (Group 1) (British Champions Series) (Entire Colts & Fillies) Class 1

[OFF 4.33]   (1m4f6y) 1m4f

For: 3-y-o **1st** £637,987.50 2nd £241,875 3rd £121,050 4th £60,300 5th £30,262.50 6th £15,187.50

1	**ADAYAR (IRE)** (1) 3 9-0 ....(107)	**Adam Kirby**
	b c by Frankel–Anna Salai (USA) (Dubawi (IRE))
	(Charlie Appleby) awkward start, soon tracked leaders on inner, pushed along and led against far rail over 2f out, ridden and clear when edged right over 1f out, soon edged left, kept on strongly final 110yds	[op 40/1] **16/1**
2	4¹/₂ **MOJO STAR (IRE)** (10) 3 9-0 .... David Egan
	b c by Sea The Stars (IRE)–Galley (Zamindar (USA))
	(Richard Hannon) held up in rear, good headway and prominent over 3f out, ridden over 2f out, edged left and went second over 1f out, kept on final 110yds, no match for winner (vet said colt was struck into on its left fore)	[op 80/1] **50/1**
3	3¹/₄ **HURRICANE LANE (IRE)** (5) 3 9-0 ....(112) William Buick
	[7³/₄] ch c by Frankel–Gale Force (Shirocco (GER))
	(Charlie Appleby) prominent, pushed along briefly halfway, pushed along over 3f out, headway and chased winner over 2f out, soon ridden, edged left and lost second over 1f out, no extra final 110yds (vet said colt lost both of its fore shoes)	[op 11/2 tchd 5/1] **6/1**
4	3¹/₄ **MAC SWINEY (IRE)** (8) 3 9-0 ....(119) Kevin Manning
	[11] (J S Bolger) dwelt start, soon midfield on outer, pushed along and headway over 3f out, ridden over 2f out, went fourth over 1f out, soon edged left and no impression	[op 13/2] **8/1**
5	nk **THIRD REALM** (2) 3 9-0 ....(108) Andrea Atzeni
	[11¹/₄] (Roger Varian) took keen hold, midfield, bumped after 2f, ridden when outpaced and lost position over 3f out, rallied over 1f out, no impression final 110yds	[op 12/1] **14/1**
6	3 **ONE RULER (IRE)** (11) 3 9-0 ....(114) James Doyle
	[14¹/₄] (Charlie Appleby) held up in rear, shaken up over 4f out, ridden and switched right 3f out, headway and hung left 2f out, soon no impression, beaten inside final furlong	[op 11/1 tchd 8/1] **17/2**
7	2³/₄ **BOLSHOI BALLET (IRE)** (9) 3 9-0 ......(117) Ryan Moore
	[17] (A P O'Brien) tracked leaders on outer, pushed along over 3f out, ridden and outpaced over 2f out, weakened over 1f out (trainer could offer no explanation for colt's performance. vet said colt was struck into on its right hind in the early stages of the race)	[tchd 6/4] **11/8F**
8	2 **YOUTH SPIRIT (IRE)** (7) 3 9-0 ....(111) Tom Marquand
	[19] (Andrew Balding) tracked leader, every chance and pushed along over 3f out, ridden and lost position over 2f out, soon weakened	**25/1**
9	1¹/₄ **JOHN LEEPER (IRE)** (12) 3 9-0 ......(106) Frankie Dettori
	[20¹/₄] (Ed Dunlop) took keen hold, held up in last, raced wide and headway 4f out, ridden and outpaced over 2f out, soon dropped to rear and struggling, beaten when edged left over 1f out	[op 7/1 tchd 7/2] **8/1**
10	³/₄ **GEAR UP (IRE)** (6) 3 9-0 ....(112) Ben Curtis
	[21] (Mark Johnston) led, pushed along over 3f out, ridden and headed over 2f out, weakened over 1f out	[op 33/1] **50/1**
11	**SOUTHERN LIGHTS (IRE)** (3) 3 9-0 ....
	[42] ....(104) Declan McDonogh
	(Joseph Patrick O'Brien) midfield, bumped after 2f, lost position when bit short of room after 4f, ridden and dropped to last over 4f out, lost touch from 3f out, tailed off	[op 33/1] **33/1**

11 ran   TIME 2m 36.85s (slow by 0.85s) **SP TOTAL PERCENT** 112

NON RUNNER: Mohaafeth(IRE)(unsuitable ground)
1st OWNER: Godolphin BRED: Godolphin
TRAINER: Charlie Appleby at Newmarket, Suffolk
2nd OWNER: Amo Racing Limited
3rd OWNER: Godolphin

TOTE WIN £18.40; PL £4.80, £7.95. £1.65; EX £608.50; CSF £629.43; TRICAST £5222.09
TRIFECTA £4766.80

DBI (SP%) L [Stalls 1-5] **69** (26%) M [6-8] **31** (16%) H [9-12] **50** (58%)

I tend to use caution when betting at festivals, although this particular meeting has always been a favourite of mine and as you can see from the tissue and result, the prices on offer were too good to miss.

marked down those tissue prices alongside every horse in your Racing Post, and then marked down the early prices alongside, exactly as I tell you to do, and then went about your busy day ahead.

You may have even had yourself a pint or two and a bite to eat before finally settling down in front of the TV with the Racing Post in which you jotted all the prices down earlier, just as the horses are going to post.

You then simply **put a line** through all runners **not** being backed according to the **Method** on the figures you have written down.

You were left with three horses that were clearly being backed for good money. Remember that Mohaafeth, being a non-runner at 7/1, affected the price structure of the race, which means Bolshoi Ballet 13/8 to 11/8 was **not** being backed, nor was Hurricane Ivor really. 7/1 to 6/1 was about right, the other 6 of the eleven runners were drifting badly, even though their odds should have been lower, again taking into consideration the reduction factor of the non-runner.

Even if you backed all three of the remaining runners 1 point each way staking six points. You would have returned over 30 points.

I cannot give you an example that is easier than that. Check the details for yourself.

EACH-WAY BETTING

You may well consider the next statement to be somewhat strange, but I urge you all **not to be ultra careful when gambling!**

Go back and read that again if you wish, because I need you to let it sink in.

The very worst punters, in my opinion, try to go down the safety path when having a bet and end up bleeding money.

Putting your money down is taking a risk, we all know that, and we should all be prepared to lose.

Scared money never wins

It makes perfect sense to me for a bookmaker to encourage each-way betting, that can feel like quite a comfort to you if your horse gets placed or touched off in a photo finish, and you do not lose your stake.

Essentially two bets are being placed, one for the horse to win, the other as an insurance if it gets beaten and finishes placed, but remember, if the horse gets left in the stalls, or underperforms for whatever reason and does not get placed, you lose both bets.

Another added fact is the price! Any less than 5/1 you lose part of your stake anyway unless you can seek out the races that offer bigger terms. Bookies are pleased to take each-way bets because it reduces their liability and doubles their turnover and, considering we have more losers than winners, it works in their favour and not ours. I do not say never, but each way only works for me if the odds present themselves.

But as strange as it seems, the **Method** does not encourage seeking out better odds, it is aimed at **winning and increasing your bank balance.**

What is the point of feeling smug securing 10/1 about an 8/1 shot if it loses? (Value seekers play a different scenario.)

The technicalities around possibility and probability in terms of value that all betting gurus will have you spend your working day on is another time-consuming way to brush up your maths, and I am not suggesting you can get away from the mathematics of gambling, I am simply pointing you in the direction that emphasises probability.

The starting points for all books sold on value in betting will probably refer to tossing a coin as the easy example of odds that are 50/50 about the coin coming down heads or tails.

If you were offered 2/1 for heads and 1/2 for tails, which one would you bet on? Obviously, for a £10 stake, heads will return you £30, and tails will return you £15, so the no-brainer is to bet on tails as the value. Based on the probability of a hundred spins, 50 will be heads and 50 will be tails. Meaning your wins at £10 stake returns you £1,500 on heads and your losses on tails were £500, leaving you with what they call in the trade 'a bag of sand' profit.

But if the coin comes down heads every time you still lose £1,000, and when you consider that the law of averages does not apply when betting, the above could be described as a load of that smelly stuff.

In fact, the real odds for a coin falling 50/50 from a hundred spins is 8% and seeing that this book promises not to get you bogged down in the technical data, we can all focus on the structure of the **Method and** work it into our betting patterns and leave the rest to the boffins.

Franklin D Roosevelt said,
I think we consider too much the good luck of the early bird and not enough the bad luck of the early worm.'

So much has been written on gambling over the decades and very little can be learnt, because with all games of chance the outcome can only be put into statistics, and yet millions of people like to gamble and risk their hard-earnt money with little or no knowledge on how to do so.

All you need when going to the casino, for example, is your wallet in one pocket, and your bus fare home in the other pocket (just to be safe), a bit of luck, and maybe some lucky heather, and you are ready to go. It is also useful to have a clear head whilst you are there, so at least you think you know what you are doing, but tipsters, programmes, or form books are not needed, you just need to go there **and hope to win!**

I find it quite shuddering to think that very same mindset is also applied with so many people who go to the races. They pay their money at the turnstile and expect something to unfold once they are inside, some magic formula will occur that wins them money. They walk around without even buying a race card or newspaper, **they just hope to win.**

I find it fascinating to watch people at race tracks trying to decide which horse to place a bet on, standing in crowds in front of the bookies, looking for that elusive clue, before scurrying back to the bar where they can get some more of that inspiration stuff that makes them cheer their heads off even if their horse finishes last. The ones who are burying their heads in the race card or newspaper two minutes before the off are only hoping the nap of the day might be in that race.

In the run-up to producing this book I took it on myself to research and ask different racegoers what they had backed, and why. It became so much of a fascinating exercise that I could easily write another book on the subject. I would simply ask someone standing next to me had they had a bet. A friendly question that most, if not all, would respond to. By and large the answers were similar… because it is favourite, or it ran well last time, or it won its last race, or it has won here before. All of which are totally and utterly useless in determining how it will run on this occasion, in fact, it is quite rare to speak to someone who is in any way knowledgeable with the racing scene.

I have had some varied replies from the women I had spoken to, such as: 'That is my daughter's name,' or' I always back Frankie,' or 'I like the colours.' Quite unbelievable if you consider how careful women are with money compared to men, that they put it down on decisions like that as if it does not count. They will back their fancy at 10/1 when it is showing at 12/1 on the bookies' pitch next door, back each way on a 6/4 favourite. Because that is what regular racegoers just do.

When I ask why, it appears the general rule is that they save up all year for their big day out and spend with gay abandon, win, or lose, so I must cut them some slack for having a good time, but I still feel annoyed they are filling the bookies' satchels even more.

I was talking to a crowd of girls having fun on the lawns at Royal Ascot and asked them what they fancied. They had each backed £10 on every horse in the 9-runner field so they were certain to collect, and the winner would buy the next bottle of bubbles.

A 5/4 shot won the race, which returned them £22.50. Enough for a small jug of Pimms, whereas the £90 staked would have bought a nice bottle of champagne.

There are, of course, the serious racegoers who study form and work hard in trying to make it pay, and some of the information I had accidentally gleaned with my research has been very useful indeed, but overall, the vast majority of those who bet have little or no idea how the industry works.

As I said, nothing feels worse than when your selection flops out of the stalls or falls at the first fence or simply does not perform, and your bet is down the tubes; each-way bets are no help here! Which is why I rarely play each way. I much prefer to spread the stake. Have my win bet and use the place money to back a second and even a third horse win bet in the same race, always depending on price.

Not only does this keep your interest in the race alive, if there is a no-show or whatever else from your 1st choice, it also supports the **Method** which regularly leaves you more than one horse to make your decision about.

The Value nuts will frown on this, but it does get results for me, and it will get results for you. Of course, we must always be aware of the girls at Ascot scenario, and only back like that when the race presents the odds for that type of bet.

Let me give you an example of a race that not only outlines my way of thinking but should give you a typically clear picture of what I am trying to get across to you the reader, steering you away from the each-way bets that present themselves as good decisions.

A valuable 10-runner handicap on the May meeting 2023 at Chester on the Friday looked a very nice race to the eye. Run over 12 furlongs on soft ground, and quite an open betting market.

Cap Francais, tissued at 14/1, was a non-runner that would slightly reduce the tissue odds of the remaining 9.

A lot of value seekers would go for the favourite and the master rider at Chester, Ryan Moore, at 11/4 and 3/1 in a race like this, although no value in each way at those odds. There was, however, a **Method** horse being smashed in the market.

Maksud, was tissued at 10/1 and mostly on offer at around 5/1. Some confidence there, without any doubt, and who could criticise anyone for making the decision to place a bet based on the price alone?

So now let us create a hypothetical and safe £10 each-way bet and let the gambling gods do the rest.

What transpired was the £20 stake being lost when the stalls opened, with Maksud flopping out of the traps and never on terms, finishing a well-beaten 7th.

Some might say, 'Well, that's racing for you, and shit happens.' What I will say, however, is give yourself a better chance with a bit more thought.

Firstly, Ryan Moore's mount was a bit too generous at the price and therefore encouragement to bet elsewhere. At parade time the odds were clear that all runners except 2 are drifting in the market (remember there was a non runner and Savvy Victory, Ryan Moore's mount, although a live runner was not backed) so the **Method** said, for the same £20 stake, bet both horses being backed to win, as follows.

Maksud	£9 stake at 5/1 returns £54
Pride Of America	£11 stake at 4/1 returns £55 WINNER

So, you can see what I am outlining here. The original decision to bet £20 looking through rose-tinted glasses would have potentially returned £80 with your £10 each-way bet.

The above way, as shown, returns £55 with a little adjustment of your stake, and for me a plus 175% profit on your total outlay is always satisfyingly good, don't you agree?

DOs AND DON'Ts

Whenever I have conversations about racing, I tend to become somewhat cautious hearing those who regularly bet tell me how successful they are at gambling, and how they win on a regular basis. There are always the after-racing discussions in the pub, and very few will declare their losses. Instead, they will bang on about how well a certain horse won and what a certainty it was, but unless they are form students spending hours studying and being ultra selective on the races they choose to bet in, I find it highly unlikely they show profits. You cannot keep going to weddings, you have to have funerals now and again, and what it also does to another gambler, is to make him feel that he is getting it wrong. They like to give you the impression they are always successful, because constant losses can be deemed as failure, though they are never quite able to back it up with any solid proof or system.

You would not ask to see their bank balance, and why should you, just ask them to share the winners with you, though do try to get the information before the race.

Remember, there is no magic formula, it does not exist, so please do not be led to thinking there is, and someone else knows it – they do not. Try and get used to using the **Method** systematically and you will grind out margins and put money in your bank instead of taking it out… But I urge you not to just use it blindly on every race. It is a massive aid that every sensible punter can use, especially with a bit of added assistance, lots of which I am listing below, and elsewhere through the book that will support the way you bet. Take another look at the proof I can give you … Wherever could you find a bookmaker stupid enough to offer you 17/2, 16/1, and 50/1 in a **three**-horse race, **and being allowed to back them each way**, because they were the three you were left with if you took the **Method** to its exact interpretation in the 2021 Derby?

BEING SELECTIVE

When I say you must not use the **Method** blindly, I can explain why.

The hundreds of horse races run on the flat each year in the UK all have class bands, which were put in place to ensure that horses of a comparable ability race against each other. What I have learnt over the years becomes a very strong point of view.

All owners want their horse to win, and trainers need winners to survive in the industry, and like any other sport there will be a league system of class and quality. And it tends not to be the top end of racing where we can be successful. The Arabs and other wealthy owners are not too bothered about the prize money on offer. They want top class horses for the breeding purposes, and therefore target the top races. The trainer's job is to target the right races and try to win them, and despite a common view with racing, there is no skulduggery to be had, especially for betting purposes.

I am not saying that the Michael Tabors or JP McManus's of the racing world do not bet, absolutely they do, but why on earth would they want to bet, say, 5k on a 2/1 shot to win 10k when the prize money is 300k and the stud value of the horse increases ten-fold?

The point being that caution is the word with group racing, and not always helpful for us and the **Method.** Yes, it can be used, as we know with the 2021 Derby, but elimination will give us a clearer picture with these races where the optimists are having a go with a highly rated horse, but having a go is usually as far as they get. It becomes pretty rare for a small trainer to bag these big pots, and the betting is often lopped sided, focussing on the top trainers running top-class thoroughbreds, bringing the form down to very fine margins and difficult from a betting perspective.

Breeding is a magical word in horse racing and carries an awful lot of weight with those who study it. Commentators and tipsters are usually well-versed on the subject, which is proven to be the pike staff of the industry and the very purpose of racing itself, but how crucial it is in finding winners for the uninitiated is debatable. So many top-class horses fail to make it at stud and the expectations of their offspring can be so very disappointing and even disastrous when betting on them. Trainers like Aidan O'Brien, who will achieve something near to 10 million pounds in prize money alone each year, have a task like no other supporting that huge operation in winner achieving. Therefore the Ballydoyle runners are usually over-bet, because they run so many unfathomable horses, such as un-raced two- and three-year-olds, and horses learning their trade, and for gambling purposes this will only cause confusion, because there is little or nothing to base our judgement on, except the fact that those behind the scenes might be spreading the word on how well a certain horse is doing on the gallops, and the market is over-reacting, or the market is being formed by breeding alone, so I find it difficult to evaluate this type of race where many of these hypes fall flat.

I have always said if reincarnation were a choice, I would want to come back as a thoroughbred stallion. These magnificent animals are pampered like babies, fed the best that money can buy, have 3 or more of the best females brought to them every day, and all they need to do is to win a couple of group races early in their career and they are made.

GROUND CONDITIONS

Most horses will have a particular ground preference that can be fundamental to its running style, so pay attention to the figures that support the ground conditions. I find the pdf printout helpful here, it shows at a glance the horse's performance on the various ground. But please check the figures you see are current; it is no good getting excited about a high figure that may have been achieved a long time ago, especially if it was over a different trip, as it sometimes is. Obviously, a horse will not perform to its maximum potential on unsuitable ground, so check if he or she has run on a certain ground condition before you decide to dismiss it. Trainers will often wait for specialist ground conditions such as firm or good to firm to run their horses but make yourself aware of the horses that act on the surface. I listened to a race presenter on tv some time back telling us that a particular horse, which I fancied, that was about to run in a competitive race at Brighton, had not won on firm ground, which in itself was a negative, but I had already checked his pedigree that suggested he would. In fact, he had never ever run on firm ground, and duly won with ease.

DISTANCE

The second most important thing is distance on the day.

Certain horses, especially those in handicaps where form is somewhat established, can be fairly specialist performers at a particular distance, though trainers will often experiment with trips different from those which the horse is bred to do. For a horse to be trying a new trip can be somewhat of a guessing game, even the trainer is never sure if it will get the new trip, but if the horse is trained to peak with conditions in its favour the **Method** will sometimes tell us the confidence behind the trainer's decision to run by seeing the horse trading lower than the tissue. On the other hand, it can be significant if the horse drifts, indicating the opposite where the horse is getting a run and some help from the handicapper, and one to follow back at his optimum trip.

Trying to be simplistic, as I always try to do, I should point you to the way that I establish the ground and distance together on the R/P web site.

Click on the race itself and select a runner that opens up the form lines. If you select the pos.finish dist / winner, at the top of the form lines it brings the winning runs, or best finishing runs, to the top of the page where you can immediately identify the horse's obvious preference for ground and distance. I find this particularly helpful when I am assessing a race, and it takes no time at all.

TRACKS/DRAW

I glean an awful lot of information from watching the replays of various races, with the understanding that cameras will often give us false impressions of a race. A jockey, for example, who is taking a wide route on a turning track is maybe looking for better ground but having to work his mount that much harder for fear of losing ground to the horses on the inside. If they tied a piece of string to both horses' tails, the one on the outside would cover many lengths more than the inside horse, and the form book reads 'beaten a length', whereas we know he would have been close to winning, had he taken an inside route, and therefore he or she could be treated as a winner without a penalty next time up. Another common error made when watching a replay of a race that clearly shows us a horse finishing well, and seeing that the camera never lies, we can assume the horse will get further based on what we see.

Camera angles in horse racing can be very deceiving, especially at tracks where the camera is not on the line. What looks to the eye like a horse far side clearly in front, when actually nearside is in front on the angle, giving the impression that nearside had finished fast as the camera angle levels up, which can truly shock you, especially if you get a view from an overhead camera as they sometimes have on the big races, and compare the two.

I highlighted earlier that I was not getting into technicalities with you, just keeping it simple in sharing the information I consider important, and I want you to be very much aware of camera angles that can over-emphasise a finishing run as a race is coming to its conclusion.

Bookies will often over-exaggerate the fact in pricing up.

The draw is something under the track heading that I never want you to underestimate the importance of.

In most flat races, if not all, the draw will help enormously when making your decision to bet, and it is not always sprint race where the draw is important. Everyone will tell you that Chester is a great example of draw number one being so important in sprint races, because of the nature of the track and its tight turns. I can tell you, however, that horses drawn one are always over bet! Although strangely, draw one does not win as many races as racegoers are led to believe, and for me, it is pace, combined with the lower draw importance, where the good jockey can claim the golden highway on the inside, therefore setting themselves up for a winning run off the home turn.

There are quite a few right-handed tracks in the UK where the draw is very important.

Ascot is another great example of how important the draw can be over a mile and a quarter, would you believe?

The right-handed track lends itself to a middle draw with the right turn that comes up quickly, again enabling the jockey to balance their mount and obtain a winning position as they reach the big swinging turn into the short straight. Wide runners burn too much energy early and inside drawn horses struggle to get a run unless they sprint early and use their energy.

I have found that other right-handed tracks such as Goodwood, over 7 furlongs and even a mile in big fields, have a strong bias… Anything drawn wide has to run much further than the lower drawn runners and use up valuable stamina needed for the finish, because they hit the turn so quickly after the start over 7 furlongs, and cannot get settled quickly enough over 8 furlongs if drawn wide.

Also, at the same track it is worth remembering the opposite applies to 5-furlong and 6-furlong sprints when assessing your form, because horses drawn low on the straight course have the same struggle in using stamina, as the runners will so often favour the stand side.

Leicester is another one, where the long sweeping turns over a mile is important for low-drawn runners to obtain that position to win without running out of valuable energy needed for the finish.

It would take weeks to describe the various advantages of the draw on every racecourse, and some are not as prevalent as others, but the point is being made to check the history of past races run, which will give you a definite edge, and draw position for past winners can be seen on the 5-year trends, shown on the pdf file under the race in question, especially factoring in the pace as well.

Essentially horse racing carries an unfair bias when positioning the stalls on a turning track that we must all evaluate when deciding to bet.

Just look at the advantage wide-drawn runners are given in athletics, for example, until they all merge together on the inside once the first lap is run. With horse racing, starting stalls are never at an angle, and wide- drawn runners unfortunately must suffer. So, when looking at replays take note how well wide-drawn runners perform, especially for next time out, and make notes. All of which will help you when making your mind up which one to back. These small decisions can and will make all the difference.

Has it ever occurred to you that all human track events are anti-clockwise? Running tracks, speed skating, track bicycle races, roller skating, even dancers and ice skaters go anti-clockwise, which is something to do with most of us humans being right-handed and right footed, giving us the comfort of stride on left-handed tracks. Our brains work that way, even aircraft go left-handed when stacking; so, too, do revolving doors move left-handed and so, too, do most horse racing tracks.

But some equine athletes prefer to run the other way round, and it is always worth a check on their preference, because we do have other right-handed tracks apart from those I have mentioned above that suit that type of animal. You can find this useful info on the form pages of the Racing Post, directly beneath the past winning performances of the horse.

PACE

Finding the pace for a horse-race can be most important to the result, even in small fields the pace can be crucial. A jockey may have a mount that front runs amidst a group of hold up horses, and he can set slow fractions for example and therefor ruin the chance of a power finisher. Always difficult to assess.

But in a big field it is near impossible for tactics to apply. This is where you can use the pdf file that gives the likely pace of the race.

For this exercise I like to jot down the draw numbers left to right on a separate piece of paper, depending on the track. Stall one is always on the furthest rail from the grandstand.

I then jot down the pace or running style that is known. Always shown on the pdf file before the horse's name.

I am not quite sure if you would decipher my scribble, so for simplicity purposes and to make this as clear as possible I have covered this in a small, printed table (see image 012 later in the book) illustrating a race that was run at Thirsk 2023 after a deluge of rain, but clearly shows the principle of draw and pace, and the betting pattern.

Importantly the **Method** is used as well. You will see in the table mentioned I have included the likely pace of the race underneath each stall number on the draw.

For speed I only write the letter L (likes to Lead) and H (a hold-up horse), the rest typically run behind the pace, mid-division or otherwise.

I then include the tissue prices, and then the subsequent prices in the columns below that.

This begins to provide a likely visual of the horses as they leave the starting stalls, showing us three important things.

The first being how the pace should unfold during the early part of the race, and which horses are likely to adopt the middle or hold-up positions.

Secondly, what lies in front of them, it may be a sharp left- or right-hand turn, where a hold-up horse cannot get a clear run and could well be boxed in, or it's a straight gallop-and-go track, that certain horses prefer. All good stuff when making final assessments.

And thirdly, how the market is reflected accordingly.

Let us say a fancied runner tissued at 6/1, for example, is drawn wide, and it is trading late at 10/1. This could be because it's sweating, or headstrong in the parade ring, but if all of those around him on the draw pattern are on the drift in some description it cannot be because they are all sweating up.

It is a clear indication the **wisdom of the crowd** is solving the draw dilemma for you, which is being factored into the market, giving you that important edge that should not be overlooked.

Equally important is the elimination factor, as used with the **Method**, which will also help when making that final decision to bet.

It would take a lot of reading to include the many races that are decided like this, and the few that I have highlighted throughout this book all carry valuable information that forms a beautiful pattern to bet.

John Mayne, a close friend of mine and racing stalwart, owned the successful sprinter Kingsgate Native, who was entered at Royal Ascot in the King's Stand Stakes after winning the Nunthorpe at York as a two- year-old ridden by Jimmy Quinn. The first two-year-old to win the Nunthorpe for 15 years.

John Best, the trainer, was quite bullish of his chances at Ascot and Jimmy Quinn kept the ride. Not much could be gleaned from the draw for the 13-runner field because it was the first day and only the second race of the meeting. The weather was great, and Kingsgate looked resplendent in the parade ring and went to post exactly as the jockey asked him to do.

As the stalls opened Jimmy did what he had done at York, which was point him and go, and immediately made for the far rail from draw 6, which turned out to be disastrous in retrospect, as the first three home were drawn 11, 9, and 12. Kingsgate finished 10th, beaten nearly five lengths under what is known as a sympathetic ride.

We all did our conkers that day and despite a special trip to Royal Ascot, the mood was gloomy. It would be a fair statement to say that we bet with our hearts, although this was not to be filed under the 'mug bet' section. He was a group horse with proven form in the book. Kingsgate was still entered in Saturday's Diamond Jubilee, Group One race, which is run over 6 furlongs. This was ideal because the Nunthorpe is a stamina requirement race, and armed with the fact that all week they were winning the straight course races on the stand side at Ascot, we went to war with the bookmakers.

Kingsgate was drawn 18 of the 20-strong field and could be backed at 40/1 plus on the exchanges. Steve Drown was given the ride and rode to the trainer's instructions perfectly, settling Kingsgate behind the leaders along the golden highway of the week, setting the race up nicely to use his finishing speed and win cosily at 33/1. He had not lost a leg, or anything like in the King's Stand race, he was still a proven group horse. It was classical DRAW bias that won the day with the next four past the post drawn 20, 17, 19, and 16. Very powerful stuff that must not be underestimated, and we all filled our boots big time.

Apart from the thrill and excitement, there was a beautiful story to be shared... Katherine, who is John Mayne's daughter-in-law, had never been to the races before. She enjoyed a champagne lunch in the owners' and trainers' lounge before racing and had a £50 win on the tote which paid £48 to a one-pound stake, winning her £2,400. She shook hands with the Queen during the presentation and she dined with us at Mayfair's fashionable Le Gavroche restaurant in the evening to round off a truly memorable day. She called John the following morning to say thank you, and that she had a wonderful day and would like to go to the races again!

When any kind of information is shared, and it is any good, the word will spread. Holiday resorts, restaurants, theatres, pubs, gyms, golf courses, medicine, in fact everything we want we seek and search and everything we hear we respond accordingly, and I think it is safe to say hundreds of factors involved with horse racing have all been discussed a thousand times before. And yet the final solution still hangs in the balance.

Books and articles have been printed, web sites created, and yet the conclusion for successful gambling according to the experts always boils down to value and mathematics. If anything becomes new in the gambling arena and is remotely successful it is soon exploited, and it will not work for long. That philosophy has been proven beyond doubt over the years, but the **Method** will hold up as long as betting itself exists, because its very existence works on not fitting the criteria of what we are led to believe in horse racing i.e., value, mathematics, or tipsters. In other words, we have a window of our own that we can look through whenever we want and make our minds up to bet or not, and that point is very important.

If your health or livelihood were in the balance, you would do what it takes to steady the ship and get a result. Well, it is the same with racing and the **Method** that I have given you, it takes a certain understanding and digestion, and the final decision from you to apply the trip, ground, track, trainer, etc, and strike.

Let me explain why it will always work… Apart from the legal requirements of Odds Layers who have a duty to display the correct odds, it has to be a somewhat level playing field for a bookmaker or Layer to do any business at all. They could not lay each horse in a race at evens, because they would not do any trade. The Bettor would go elsewhere, so they must price up accordingly and fall in line with the market, which I have mentioned is now controlled by the exchanges, and then adjust those prices with the various fluctuations up to the off. To shortchange you, as they usually do at dog tracks, they must work to bigger margins, bringing the over round in line with everyone else who is trading. Much like a market trader trying to sell tomatoes for £4 a kilo when most others are selling at £2 a kilo.

So, when a real gamble is taking place at horse racing, how could they possibly hide it without filling their book up with potential winning bets by laying the higher price? In simple terms they must run for cover and reduce the odds on the gamble, and by doing so they have to push the others out in the betting to level the over round.

Reducing odds is nothing new to explain, in fact it is obvious. I suggest **no one** has ever used the **Method** before in the way that I insist you do religiously every time you bet on horse racing, and if you simply back the horses that are seemingly being backed then continue to do so, all the ingredients are the same, the same horses, the same conditions, the same jockeys and the same bookmakers taking your money.

SILENCE IN COURT

A more simplistic explanation that I could give you might be described as a court house that has a jury of 12 people (**wisdom of the crowd**) whose job it is to listen carefully and intently to all of the relevant information (**read the form**) laid out by the case (**horse race**) in question, and come up with a final decision.

Of course, the jury sometimes get it wrong (**lose**) and the wrong person is convicted (**another horse wins**) but overall, the court room is a system (**the Method**) like no other that is proven unequivocally in making the correct decision.

When the betting exchanges were first introduced to the mainstream, they were pitched against the age-old principle of betting. That is, put your money down and, if you win, go and collect.

The selling point with exchanges, however, was the opposite, because you could bet that a horse would lose. A concept that seemed incredibly attractive to the uninitiated but proved to be an extremely dangerous one.

Anyone who has ever had a bet would tell you that it is easier to back a loser than a winner, though looking at it from another angle the downside can be horrific, especially against the rewards.

You are essentially becoming the bookmaker when laying a horse. In other words, you accept the bet offered, and keep the stake if it loses. Trouble is, it becomes a mini war with the crowd, where 5/1, say, is offered by the bookmaker and 11/2 or bigger will be offered on the exchange. This is how the market moves in a certain direction, as I have explained earlier, bringing the ones with the best chances of winning to being backed, and those with little hope drifting.

This is now reflected by the bookmakers in their own structure with automation that brings everyone in line with each other and unwittingly supporting the **Method**. 8/1 shots become 12/1, 12/1 shots become 16/1, 20/1 shots become 33/1, 33/1 shots become 100/1 and 7/1 shots become 4/1... The jury is working in making its decision, the news is leaking before the final verdict is given, a fifteen-runner race is now reduced to four! Time to move in and make our own adjustments (ground, draw, trip, etc) and bet ... not guilty (**winner**) becomes the overall majority.

FOOLS RUSH IN

Take caution when looking on any exchange site early in the day when checking the odds, it will reflect the basic Racing Post prices, with a few minor discretions. This is quite the norm, but do not rush in with a bet at that point if there is one that shows much lower. It may well be the start of a gamble, though chances are it is not, because there will be very little monies bet at that point, and it may well fizzle out as the market gathers pace. Take time to check how much is bet, (it is always displayed somewhere). It will be 5 or 6 percent of the final amount with little or no indication for you to place that early bet. If you do not know already, the left-hand columns are the layers (bookmakers) prices, and the right-hand columns are the bettors' prices being offered.

I find it interesting, however, with these early morning markets, as they enable you to see a somewhat different picture of the market movement, and – apologies for using another analogy – fishing is the best explanation I can give.

It is like throwing some bait into the pool and finding out what interest there is, further highlighting the importance of the exercise. We lose our money if we get it wrong… the fish lose their life!

On screen you will see the prices in the lefthand column that the layers are offering with always the stake included as one, so a horse on offer on screen at 4/1 is actually 3/1. If that price stays, there for a while it may well be lengthened to 4.5 (7/2) but just look underneath that price of the amount available to bet and it is generally £1 or £2 only.

All of this is computer-orchestrated and endorses the reason behind it. No one wants to lay a horse for £500 say at 3/1 if they can lay it at 2/1, but gradually the stakes will increase and become bigger and bigger until the strike. However, if the layer (fisherman) does not get any interest he will move to another spot (**try another horse**) or change the bait (**offer bigger odds**).

The right-hand column, that we can see on screen early doors, is showing no real reflection of the final market. These prices on offer early in the day are very much bigger than the left-hand column and usually carry a much bigger stake underneath the odds, because this punter is happy to buy a horse early at a much-inflated price, so they can sell it back (lay it) later when the market is correct. Again, fishing for business and trying to explore the edge he might have in doing so.

Overall, the exchanges are a very established part of the gambling system and here to stay. It did seem obvious in the early days that exchanges would be forced out of the gambling arena by the strength of the bookmakers combined, for encroaching on their business. But bookmakers were happy to live alongside these new giants where they can offload a liability with them, with no danger to themselves, because the bookies' odds are ALWAYS lower than those on the exchanges for that very reason. They can buy those over-inflated odds themselves.

So, the bookie with a good clerk who accepts a bet, say £100 on a 33/1 shot, has a liability of £3,300. He then buys it for £70 on the exchange at 50/1. His liability has now been scrapped. He has £30 profit, if the horse loses, and £200 profit if it wins. In the pre-exchange days, he might be the only one offering 33s and he would have to suffer and hold the hot potato and pay out the £3,300 if it wins.

But remember, if you consider laying a horse yourself, say a 4/1 shot with Ladbrokes, you will have to lay 9/2 or 5s to get matched, risking x5 times your stake, and sore balls if it wins. But what you are really doing is backing every other horse in the race which no way fits in with the **Method,** and I need you to be clear about what you are doing.

IN SUMMARY

I will not bore you with the vast number of winners achieved by the **Method** as I consider by now you will have made your mind up for yourselves, or thrown this book in the bin, declaring it as 'a load of rubbish'. Before you do that, let me remind you of the Derby result 2021 for reasons I need you to understand. Firstly, when deciding to write this book I realised that it would have undoubtably brought interest to a whole heap of people who know little or nothing about horse racing, so I needed a base to set my stall out on. It would be no good speaking about a seller at Catterick or a maiden at Redcar. It needed to be something that everyone would associate with, and what better race than the Epsom Derby.

In fact, that particular race was very much a financial success for me, it became my inspiration to bring this book together and share it with others.

(Yes, I have been slow in getting it to press and although the information refers to 2021, it is absolutely and entirely relevant.)

The Derby is the Cup Final of football, the British Open of golf, the Wimbledon of tennis; need I go on? So, the 2021 Derby was my decision, which just happens to prove the **Method** quite brilliantly in every detail.

There is always a fear, of course, when things like this happen for those who may turn to the next year's Derby meeting at Epsom and want to point out that it was a one-trick pony. So, let us look how the **Method** fared on that Derby card…

Race 1 won by Swilcan Bridge   R/P Tissue 12/1 won at 7/1

Race 2 won by Bashrikova   R/P Tissue 11/4 won at 2/1

Race 3 won by Megallan   R/P Tissue 6/1 won at 9/2

Race 4 won by Tees Spirit   R/P Tissue 10/1 won at 10/1

The Derby won by Desert Crown   R/P Tissue 7/4 won at 5/2

Race 6 won by Midnight Legacy   R/P Tissue 11/2 won at 3/1

Race 7 won by Mr Wagyu   R/P Tissue 12/1 won 12/1

Incidentally, the 2023 Derby results were also very containable for the **Method** followers, although somewhat of a different marketplace for some reason? Maybe the bookies had bigger fish to fry sorting out the Cup Final business on the same day, but none the less out of the eight races, we had 6 live winners! Once again.

These results did not just happen to please the writer of this book. It further endorses the power in the **Method**, although I would not whole-heartedly twist your arm to get too heavily involved with any of the festival meetings, for some noticeably clear and obvious reasons.

It is perfectly understandable that all owners and all trainers will want to pick up a big prize, and sending a two-year-old to run in the Norfolk stakes at Royal Ascot after it won at Beverly, for example, could well be an ego trip for a small trainer to please the owner, and so many of these hopefuls fall by the wayside, and the hype or trainer's dream comes to nothing.

If a horse finishes well and looks good to the eye, it goes into most people's notebooks, and this is great for the bookie who makes it a short price for its next race, even though the track and ground and distance may be different from its last run. Whilst it may be encouragement for the owner of a horse to be placed first time up, ask yourself how many of the other runners were out for an education? Which makes it difficult to assess their true ability, and for me, the novice, 2- and 3-year-old races are not great betting propositions (see page 76).

There will undoubtably be critics out there who do not agree with me, including those who absolutely know all about the racing game, but can never quite guide you in the right direction before the racing begins. The facts of what I have spelt out for you cannot be dismissed and if you are slightly unsure about anything let me further clarify some of the finer points.

Elimination is almost as strong as the **Method** when evaluating form. It gives you the shortlist from which to work. If you are looking for 33/1 winners when gambling, they can be rare to find. They do exist and happen, as we all know, but it is never a foundation to build on. Bookies will keep your interest alive by offering outsiders at understandable odds.

The wisdom of the crowd, however, will reflect the true odds of such horses and you can find those same horses trading at huge odds on the exchanges because they just do not stand a chance on form. We are not talking about freak results that do occur every now and again. (Remember Buster Douglas beating Mike Tyson) I am saying that a good good-un will always beat a bad bad-un...Generally!

And if an unfashionable trainer has a bit of a dark horse who is doing very well at home, why would he unleash it at somewhere like Royal Ascot, against all that cream? He would have to compete with all those clever trainers. You only need to look at the top list of trainers over the last ten years… Aidan O' Brien, Charlie Appleby, Sir Michael Stoute, William Haggas, John and Thady Gosden, etc.

So, if the cream trainers come to the top, why wouldn't the cream horses? If there is a dark one lurking from a moderate stable, and bursting to show

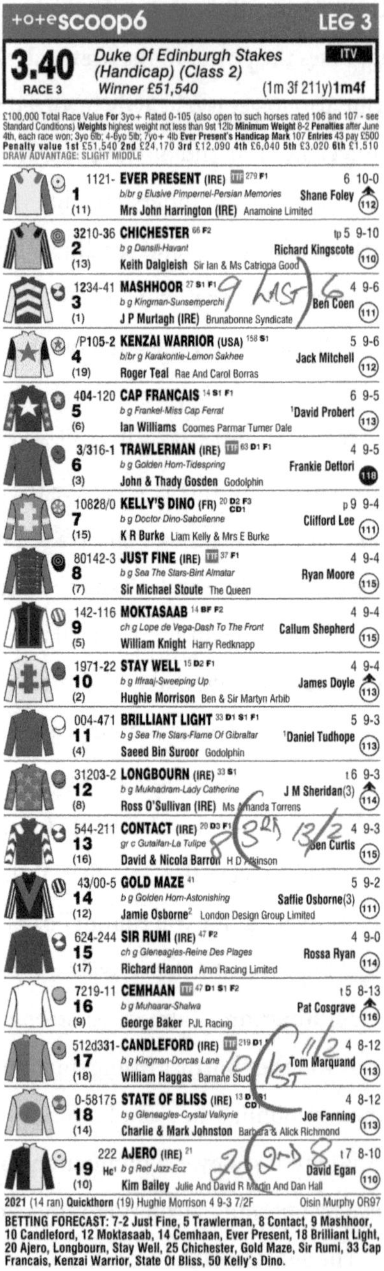

Image 007. Initially 4 horses fit the method.

After the elimination process, Candleford showed a good field a clean pair of heels.

the **Method** off, will he succeed or just give his edge away?

William Haggas, a masterful trainer, laid one out in the Duke of Edinburgh Stakes on the Friday of Royal Ascot 2022 (see Image 007).

The ground suited Candleford, who had won a novice at Windsor on fast ground as a three-year-old, achieving a handicap rating of 85. He was then gelded and tried on wrong ground at Newmarket. He ran in two mile-and-a-half races on the all-weather, winning the last of them before being put to bed to run at Ascot 219 days later. Haggas now knows that he gets the trip and had the fast ground he needs. It was officially good to firm at Ascot. The 10/1 tissue on the morning was reduced by half at post time. Candleford (returned 11/2) won going away by 6 lengths that could have been ten!

The **Method** on that particular race left you with four runners:

Mashoor tissued at 9/1 opened at 6/1 who clearly wanted soft ground and easy to eliminate (finished last).

Ajero tissued at 20/1 opened at 8/1 became a serious runner. So closer inspection was needed.

Ajero's best form was on soft and good too soft over the jumps and not ideal here, added to the fact Ajero was trained by Kim Bailey who had sent only one horse to the royal meeting in the last ten years that was unplaced, and although an excellent trainer, Kim and his team were swimming in unfamiliar and much deeper waters here.

Nonetheless a very live runner, and a small each-way stake at that price would certainly be approved and in keeping with the **Method,** simply on the huge tissue reduction (ran well, into 2nd place).

Contact was tissued at 8/1 opened at 13/2 but had lost his edge for winning a race like this, by winning his last two races, (gone up 11 pounds in the handicap) and trained by David and Nicola Barron who had never run a horse at the Royal meeting before. Contact finished third.

If a trainer runs a horse where he considers he has a stone in hand the **Method** will reflect that in some way, but please take note of the trainer and jockey and the ballpark they are playing in – some statistics will truly shock you. So not only keep up to date with current trainer form, daily lists can be found in the R/P, but also check if they have winners at that particular track.

Further to the Ascot race, Ajero was obviously a class act who was exposed at Ascot but won easily at Goodwood next up.

Also, when making your decisions from a betting perspective, I would steer you away from the 2- and 3-year-old maiden heats, and novice races. These are races with horses trying to win for the first time and the form is generally weak, and a glimmer of hope from a recent run is often exaggerated by the bookmakers and the prices they chalk up. The bookies will hang their hats on what they can, especially for the regulars who will bet just because a horse is favourite. I treat these races with severe caution because you cannot find an edge apart from the obvious that is there for all to see. There is very often a dark one lurking, like an alligator beneath the surface and ready to strike with no warning.

Group races can carry a different kind of caution with more hype than hope, especially with those horses who have shown their counterparts a clean pair of heels in lower contests and moving up the ranks. They can easily be found out when they tackle seasoned campaigners for the first time. I am not saying that a low-rank trainer should be dismissed when assessing a group race, I am simply saying that every trainer is searching for that big winner, and some will push the buttons a bit too early, and the competition can be transparent to the trainers with group horse experience.

If you refer back to Image 001. This shows a 1-page example of the Racing Post pdf files that I find comprehensive with their information on each racing meeting of the day.

I print these sheets and select the races I want to bet in, especially as it shows, at-a-glance, some of the essential information I need to bet.

On the top of each race, it gives the race conditions, class and prize value with the day's ground forecast. Reading from left to right we have: race card number, draw position, current form figures, the running style, horse name, days since last run, course or distance winner or both, beaten favourite signal, trainer, current form percentage, course runners and winners,14-day trainer form, age, weight, ground conditions with performance figures, distance and performance figures, official handicap rating, current and master speed figures, current and master R/P figures, jockey, tissue price. The other useful information given below the race itself only appears with established races, giving you the results with the relevant info of age, draw, trainer, jockey, etc, etc.

You will no doubt use the pdf information to suit your own system of winner selection and, used alongside the **Method** and **Elimination** process, it becomes an extremely powerful tool in your armour.

This info can be far more speedy and less time-consuming than trawling through the form online, and used properly its simplicity is invaluable.

Let us view in detail the 5-furlong Garrard handicap at Ascot on King George Day 2022, 5 furlongs on good to firm going (see image 008). A race I went to war with.

We can see clearly that favourites have a very poor record, 1 winner from 10, and the joint favs were uneasy in the market.

3-year-olds also have a poor record, winning just 1 from 18.

The Method Gave us 5 horses that were being backed.

Hurricane Ivor	tissued at 12/1	in to 7/1
King of Stars	tissued at 9/1	in to 8/1
Live In The Moment	tissued at 14/1	in to 9/1
Call Me Ginger	tissued at 14/1	in to 12/1
Lynn's Boy	tissued at 25/1	in to 22/1

Seemingly a difficult scenario with perhaps too many horses to evaluate. Or is it?

These prices were too exciting to pass up.

Just look carefully on what I am trying to put in your mind's eye when we take the **Method** to its full interpretation.

Here we are, presented with a five-runner race with mouth-watering prices on offer that would show a profit if you backed them all for small money. Not that I am suggesting such a daft move. I am simply presenting you with a view that is head-scratchingly good in your favour, added to the fact that we have still to work on the other important step and complete the **Elimination** process to put our gamble in place.

No winner had carried more than 9/4 in the last 5 years and Hurricane Ivor (9/11) clearly wants soft and is therefore easy to dismiss.

Lynn's Boy is 11 pounds out of the handicap, and mostly all credentials wrong. In fact, here for a day out and absolutely no chance.

Call Me Ginger…All credentials fit except a small doubt over trip, (prefers 6 furlong) though top speed is miles the best and Ascot is a very stiff track.

King Of Stars …obviously a live runner.

Live In The Moment …interesting runner though no wins on g/firm and trainer form here is poor.

So, I was left with three horses and backed them all, staking 8 points:

5 points win on Call Me Ginger, with the very capable Amie Waugh riding,

5·20 Garrard Handicap (Class 2)   £60,000 Total Race Value SKY   5f   GD-FM

For 3yo+ Weights highest weight not less than 10st Minimum weight 8-4, 3-y-o 8-2 Penalties after July 16th, each race won, 3yo 6lb; 4-6yo 5lb; 7yo+ 4lb; NOTE: Any horse rated above 110 shall initially be treated as having that rating and the highest weight allotted shall be 9st 12lb. subsequently, the excess over 110 in any rating shall be allotted to that horse without limitation to the highest weight to be carried Weight for age 3 from 4yo+ 4lb Penalty value 1st £30,924 2nd £14,502 3rd £7,254 4th £3,624 5th £1,812 6th £906

No	(Draw)	Form Figures	Horse	Age-Wt	Trainer	Jockey	OR***	FP-Rating
1	(8)	4907/9-2521	Mountain Peak	9-12	E Walker	Ryan Moore	108	115 / 115
2	(4)	2749/118-09	Hurricane Ivor	9-11	W Haggas	Tom Marquand	107	57 / 116
3	(9)	4907/1130-0	Orazam	9-1	G Boughey	William Buick	101	108 / 113
4	(7)	4907/684-42	Bond Chairman	9-0p	B Smart	Graham Lee	100	115 / 116
5	(5)	5171/884020	King Of Stars	8-9p	M Appleby	Silvestre De Sousa	95	94 / 117
6	(2)	4907/223114	Lovely Mana	8-7p	G Boughey	Saffie Osborne (3)	95	114 / 114
7	(6)	4617/6-0878	Jawwaal	8-6b	M Dods	Sam James	88	99 / 118
8	(3)	4693/770848	Live In The Moment	8-4	A West	Hollie Doyle	88	103 / 116
9	(1)	5253/005136	Call Me Ginger	8-4	J Goldie	Amie Waugh (5)	86	109 / 114
10	(10)	5716/-13236	Lynns Boy	8-4	J Butler	Rhain Ingram (3)	86	90 / 106

AGE GROUPS: 3yo 1-3-18, 4yo+ 9-17-110
FATE OF FAVOURITES: 5252566154
TRAINERS IN THIS RACE (w-pl-r): Bryan Smart 1-0-2, Ed Walker 1-0-3, Jim Goldie 1-0-3, Michael Dods 0-1-2

winning easily

2 points win on King of Stars, a gallant 2nd not quite handling the ground (possible 18 points return)

And 1 point win on Live in The Moment who ran well in third (possible 10 points return)

The staking I thought was correct for that heat, returning me 65 points and winning 57 points, although I could have played safe with a reduced stake of 6 points backing all 3 of them, all for 1 point each way, making a worst-case scenario that almost doubles my total stake. A profit is always acceptable, I agree, but these decisions to win good pots with sensible staking are the very essence of gambling.

Again, I have not just selected a race because I won a chunk of money on it, I wanted to further

Image 008. 10 runners reduced to 3, with simple form descriptions to evaluate, backing all 3.

endorse the **Method** and winner finding without the stacks of form books. These are facts that I am sharing with you the reader without the ulterior motive of charging you for the use of. You have already purchased this book so nothing extra is in it for me. I just hope you understand the **Method** and use it to its full potential without cutting any corners.

USEFUL TOOLS

I have mentioned that most of you have your own way of betting or gambling, and I realise that you are not likely to reform completely and take on board the **Method** as it is spelt out. That is your decision, but the clever ones out there who decide to make the small investment, i.e. computer, R/P subscription, and follow yours truly, or at least give it a go, may well like to follow some of the lines that I like using myself, which helps the elimination process and gets you to that final decision to place that winning bet.

Now you are, let us say in the R/P club, you can access the profiles which can be found when you click on the same page as the pdf race card file.

The profiles take away the laborious searching pages to highlight certain details of a horse such as ground preference, course preference, field size, weight, etc. It is all there with every horse, and as much as you need. Take a look and browse for ten minutes or so and give yourself an understanding on how to use that information.

Another very useful tool is the ten-year trends to be found around the pages of the race cards in the R/P itself. I use this a lot, especially with valuable races or festival meetings where it can highlight the type of age or weight or draw usually required to win that race. I had a nice touch at Glorious Goodwood 2021, I remember, with two fancied horses carrying 9/12 and 9/11 respectively running over the 2-mile 5-furlong contest on the Friday. The trends showed us that the highest winning weight carried over this extreme trip during the past ten years was 9/10, but on the hottest day I can remember at Goodwood, carrying weight like that would have been a small miracle if they outshone the trends, so I laid them both in the place market on Betfair. Both were outpaced at the business end of the race, finishing 5th and 11th respectively.

Nowhere in this book have I pushed you towards hours of study or working like a busy accountant, but trends are always worth a quick check for the information that sticks out like a sore thumb. Familiarise yourself with the at-a-glance form pages alongside the profiles and it will help enormously with that final decision. You have to sit up and take notice perhaps, where an inside draw has not happened in all those years and may well fit into the **Method** you are working on for a particular race, making the final elimination process easy for you.

With the Nunthorpe race at York 2022, one of the best sprint races of the season, the trends worked easy.

First off, the **Method** left you with five horses, which were:

Royal Acclaim, Platinum Queen, Dragon Symbol, Emaraaty Ana, and Highfield Princess.

Royal Acclaim, a three-year-old, was the favourite at 5/2… The caution for me was three-year-olds carry a poor recent record in the Nunthorpe and last year was the first winner in ten years.

Platinum Queen, a 2-year-old, although well-backed, had a mountain to climb on stats and was even easier to dismiss, with only two 2-year-old winners in modern history. Which now left the 3 runners that became dangerous to eliminate on all visible information, with prices that allowed me to back all of them.

I bet 10 points on the race... 6 points win Highfield Princess, tissued 9/1 opened 6/1 (further backed to 5/1). Won easy.

1 point E/W Emaraaty Ana tissued at 14/1 backed in to 12/1. Placed in 3rd.

1 point E/W Dragon Symbol, Tissued 25/1 backed to 20/1. Finished 5th. The race won me a total of 36 points.

Staking is important and checking on what bookies are offering is also important to establish before placing your bets.

As I have said earlier, I rarely play each way, but when opportunity presents itself with big prices when backing two or 3 horses in a race, and when bookies offer increased terms, it is a no-brainer. Lots of firms were offering first 4 on the Nunthorpe and a quarter odds a place.

Incidentally, Highfield Princess picked up another group 1 race at the Currah three weeks after the York race, on soft ground, (tissue 2/1 returning 5/4) further endorsing the form with Dragon Symbol who ran 5th again, indicating that speed and stamina is a strong pointer to group sprint races, and further supporting the **Method,** and the market move at York, because she had winning form prior to York over further, so connections knew what they were doing.

POSTMORTEMS AND PERCENTAGES

One of the enjoyable pleasures when going to the track is the postmortems and the day's events over dinner, as is often the case at Del Rio's in York, and listening to the hard luck stories, etc. We all have them, but gamblers will often tell you when asked the question whether they won today, that they backed a couple of winners, which in itself sounds good, although quite meaningless if they did not show a profit.

If you back two winners, for example at level stakes both at 2/1, say £20 on each winning £80, and have level stakes through the 7-race card, you walk out of the track losing £20. Staking is integral to your betting bank, so try to set targets and quit when you reach it. There is no strong instruction on how to stake, it is personal to how you want to bet. What is important, however, is that you give yourself a chance to win, and bet to your own values, and not someone else's.

A sensible approach is to put whatever you feel is right for you into your betting bank and only bet, say, 5% of the bank each time you place a bet. And if backing two or three in the same race, split the stakes accordingly to the odds. That way as you increase the bank value the 5% becomes bigger, winning more, but losses always stay at 5% of your bank balance.

For what it is worth in context to this book, the overround or bookmakers' percentages are shown here that I have based on the 2021 Epsom Derby – a race that has been spoken about in detail.

First let me highlight the simplicity of percentages by explaining that in betting parlance the percentage is based on 100, and therefore a 50/1 shot is 2% of 100, a 25/1 shot is 4% of a hundred, or an 8/1 shot is 12.50% of a 100, and so on.

Below is the finishing order of the 2021 Derby, the starting prices of each horse, and the percentage breakdown alongside each runner.

Adayar	16/1	6.25%
Mojo Star	50/1	2.00%
Hurricane Lane	6/1	16.67%
Mac Swiney	8/1	12.50%
Third Realm	14/1	7.14%
One Ruler	17/2	11.76%
Bolshoi Ballet	11/8	42.11%
Youth Spirit	25/1	4.00%

John Leeper	8/1	12.50%
Gear Up	50/1	2.00%
Southern Lights	33/1	3.03%

Percentage added up = 119.96%

As you can see, the total percentage on that race added up is 119.96%
Which means in simple terms that the bookmakers put £120 in their satchels, giving them a £20 profit for every £100 they pay out.

Importantly for this exercise I want you to focus on the percentages for a moment and understand the importance of the non-runners that I have been careful to point out earlier in this book.

If for example Mojo Star becomes a non-runner the book will be 2.00% shorter, meaning the bookmaker's profit margin would become 117.96%. Which would probably be acceptable in a fluctuating market without any real need for price reduction to the other runners. But take out, say, Hurricane Lane, at 16.67% the book is reduced to 103.29% making around a 3.00% profit margin for the book, not enough profit, and they would have to reflect that difference by reducing the other runners' prices accordingly, and it is these price reductions that look like other horses are being backed, whereas it is merely the bookmaker levelling his book and his profit margin.

There is no need to be that intricate or exact in your configurations but understanding these differences will become obvious to you the reader when you write the tissue price down. So, include the non-runner price on your original runner sheet, whether it be the Racing Post page or the pdf before you put the line through that non-runner.

The draw which is shown on the second column of the pdf printout is massively important in most flat races, and not only in sprint races, and always important to remember the low draw (stall 1) is nearest the inside rail and usually the furthest stall away from the stands. (Even at Chelmsford racetrack stall one is on the inside rail even though the stands are on the inside of the track.)

I highlighted earlier in the book that low numbers over 7 and 8 furlongs at Goodwood have a great advantage, and how well the high numbers perform over the straight course.

The Golden Mile Handicap is always a cracking race at the Glorious Goodwood meeting, especially on fast ground as it usually is, and last year (2022) in that race 18 runners went to post. Orbaan was the 20/1 easy **Method** winner (tissued at 25/1) drawn 2, beating Blue For You at 15/2, the other **Method** horse (tissue 9/1) drawn 1. In fact, 5 of the first 6 home were drawn in single figure boxes.

Please note: Although we can gain so much from statistical patterns in horse racing, I think it is advisable to apply caution with all regular patterns of statistics when the ground changes severely. Especially on undulating tracks such as Goodwood Epsom Catterick etc

The 6-furlong sprint on the same day at Goodwood was won by Rumstar, drawn 16 (backed from 25/1 into 22/1) but importantly the first 5 home of the 16-strong field were drawn in double figures.

Incidentally, they gave Rumstar a run on the all-weather at Kempton after the Goodwood win over 6 furlongs, opening at 12/1 drifting out to 25/1 and finishing fourth. But early autumn at Newmarket back on turf they got stuck in again 12/1 in to 8/1 over a tough 5-furlong trip, that we all knew he could handle with ease. The high draw (12), again proving important, the second was drawn 11 of the 12 runners. These are just examples of the statistics that become useful when assessing a race, and usually based on pace that I am always keen to point your way.

Big field sprint handicaps, for example, would frighten the regular punter, but I really like these races and find the challenge exciting. Quite simply these head-scratchers will look more difficult than they are, and the reason behind that is because most punters have never bothered to work a plan and find a starting point.

So, as I mentioned earlier when talking about pace, with the info I have in front of me on the pdf sheet, I will first write down the draw on a separate sheet of paper. Next, I write the pace of every horse under the stall they a drawn in.

For example: H (usually held-up) P (likes to run up with pace) M (middle pace runner) L (likes to lead).

This gives me a clear view of how the race *should* unfold.

I then jot down the tissue prices under each horse followed by up-to-date odds. I can see immediately now a finisher horse that may be buried amongst big-priced horses who like to keep up with the pace, they do all the donkey work for the finisher to swallow them up.

Or maybe there is a lone runner who usually wins by leading the field in amongst a bunch of slow hold-up runners around him where he can claim an unassailable lead.

A late-season sprint race at Doncaster springs to mind that I would like to take you through in detail (see Images 009, 010 & 011).

The race in question was a 12-runner affair on heavy ground and two horses were taken out because of the ground, leaving 10 to go to post.

The tissue for the non-runners were 6/1 and 66/1 respectively, so the reduction factor in the market would be minimal, bringing in the tissue prices slightly.

12.50 Download The BetGoodwin App Wentworth Stakes (Listed Race) (Class 1) — £40,000 Total Race Value TV4 — 6f 2y — HEAVY

For 3yo+ which have not won a Group 1 Pattern race after March 31st, 2022. Weights colts & geldings 9st 5lb; fillies 9st 3lb; of a Group 3 race 5lb: of a Group 2 race 7lb. Penalty value 1st £22,684 2nd £8,600 3rd £4,304 4th £2,144 5th £1,076 6th £540. Penalties after March 31st, 2022, a winner of a Listed race

Racecard No.	Form	Horse	Trainer	Weight	Jockey
1 (9)	82761 4-4816	Art Power	T Easterby	9-10	David Allan
2 (11)	83847 621161 F	Chipstead	R Teal	9-5	Frederick Larson
3 (3)	7849 0U1223	Commanche Falls	M Dods	9-5 p	Connor Beasley
4 (1)	8460 302081	Marshal Dan	Mrs H Main	9-5	Joshua Bryan
5 (2)	7862 3-5172	Rhythm Master	J Horton	9-5 v	P J McDonald
6 (5)	7849 941512	Summerghand	D O'Meara	9-5 v	Daniel Tudhope
7 (8)	7348 810050	Volatile Analyst	K Dalgleish	9-5 h	Jason Watson
8 (6)	8290 752212	Cherish	A Carroll	9-0 v	Mollie Phillips
9 (12)	8073 145355	Cuban Breeze	P D Evans	9-0 v	Darragh Keenan
10 (4)	8592 433117	Fast Response	K Burke	9-0	Clifford Lee
11 (7)	21640-	Fiduciary	Jane Chapple-Hyam		–
12 (10)	8592 021321	Tarrib	W Haggas	9-0	Jim Crowley

FORM   WINNER
21   173652   King's Lynn
20   712311   Dakota Gold
18   524943   Dorjan Triumphant
17   2-2015   Dream Of Dreams
16   144262   Growl

AGE GROUPS: 3yo 1-7-30, 4yo+ 8-10-97
FATE OF FAVOURITES: 014415101
TRAINERS IN THIS RACE (W-p/-r): Michael Dods 1-2-6, Keith Dalgleish 0-1-3

The **Method** left us with four horses and a live runner. Top to bottom we had Art Power, who traded at 15/8 from a 9/4 tissue. Six wins to his name though **never** run on heavy, plus the fact the 15/8 was just about right with the non-runners considered, so he was not being backed. Chipstead, the live runner, had never contested a listed race before and on his only previous run on heavy, he was beaten out of sight. Easy to dismiss.

It was also easy to see at first glance why Rhythm Master was trading lower than he should have been. He' had 10 runs in stake races with his previous trainer, but surely shooting at the moon. He ran 2nd in one such event but that was over 7 furlongs and on good to soft ground. This was

Image 009.

a completely different ballpark, and although he had won an egg-and-spoon race and an all-weather handicap, his only previous run on heavy was uninspiring to say the least, finishing 13 of 15 runners. He also wanted further than 6 furlongs.

Which now left us with two: Fast Response and Tarhib.

Fast Response was no stranger to these conditions and her previous wins on soft and heavy supported her claims here. Tarhib was the only other runner who was backed heavily with form on similar ground. But on closer inspection she had finished down the field in this race 12 months ago, with the trainer's explanation for the poor run being the soft ground.

So now what we were left with, was how would the pace pan out? Cuban Breeze was

Image 010.

A 12 runner race reduced to 10 with so much dead wood and no hopers, essentially reduced to 2. Get in !

THE METHOD

12.50 Download The BetGoodwin App
[OFF 12.55] **Wentworth Stakes (Listed Race) Class 1** (6f2y) 6f

For: 3-y-o and up 1st £22,684 2nd £8,600 3rd £4,304 4th £2,144 5th £1,076 6th £540

1 FAST RESPONSE (IRE) (4) 3 9-0 ....(95) Clifford Lee
b f by Fast Company (IRE)–Deemah (IRE) (Iffraaj)
(K R Burke) *midfield, smooth headway over 2f out, pushed along to lead over 1f out, kept on strongly inside final furlong*
[op 12/1] **8/1**

2 2 **TARHIB (IRE)** (10) 4 9-0 ......(97) Jim Crowley
b f by Dark Angel (IRE)–Allez Alaia (IRE) (Pivotal)
(William Haggas) *slowly away and bumped rival start, towards rear, going easily over 2f out, ridden and headway over 1f out, chased winner inside final furlong, made no impression*
[op 10/3] **3/1**

3 2¼ **ART POWER (IRE)** (9) 5 9-10 ......(114) David Allan
[4¼] gr h by Dark Angel (IRE)–Evening Time (IRE) (Keltos (FR))
(Tim Easterby) *slowly away and bumped rival start, raced in last, shaken up before halfway, switched right and headway over 2f out, went third inside final furlong, no match for first two (jockey said horse missed the break)*
[op 5/2] **15/8F**

4 2¼ **MARSHAL DAN (IRE)** (1) 7 9-5 ......(89) Joshua Bryan
[6½] (Heather Main) *led, ridden over 2f out, hung right and headed over 1f out, no extra inside final furlong*
[op 50/1] **66/1**

5 1¼ **COMMANCHE FALLS** (3) 5 9-5 p ...(112) Connor Beasley
[7¾] (Michael Dods) *midfield, pushed along before halfway, ridden over 2f out, some headway over 1f out, made no telling impression*
[op 9/2] **15/2**

6 5 **RHYTHM MASTER (IRE)** (2) 4 9-5 v (103) P J McDonald
[12¾] (James Horton) *prominent, pushed along over 2f out, ridden and weakened over 1f out*
[op 7/1] **11/2**

7 1¾ **CUBAN BREEZE** (12) 4 9-0 v ....(90) Darragh Keenan
[14½] (David Evans) *pressed leader, ridden over 2f out, weakened over 1f out*
[op 50/1] **125/1**

8 5½ **VOLATILE ANALYST (USA)** (8) 5 9-5 h (97) Jason Watson
[20] (Keith Dalgleish) *always towards rear*
[op 25/1] **28/1**

9 6½ **CHIPSTEAD** (11) 4 9-5 ......(103) Frederick Larson
[26½] (Roger Teal) *prominent, pushed along over 2f out, ridden and weakened over 1f out (trainer said colt was unsuited by the Heavy, Soft in places going and would prefer a sounder surface)*
[op 5/1] **9/1**

10 15 **FIDUCIARY** (7) 5 9-0 ......David Egan
[41½] (Jane Chapple-Hyam) *in touch with leaders, ridden halfway, weakened over 2f out (trainer said mare was unsuited by the heavy, soft in places going and would prefer a sounder surface)*
[op 28/1] **80/1**

10 ran **TIME** 1m 17.11s (slow by 6.81s) **SP TOTAL PERCENT** 115
NON RUNNERS: Summerghand(IRE)(self certificate), Cherish(FR)(self certificate)
1st OWNER: Nick Bradley Racing 39 BRED: Deemah Syndicate
TRAINER: K R Burke at Middleham Moor, N Yorks
2nd OWNER: Shadwell Estate Company Ltd
3rd OWNER: King Power Racing Co Ltd
TOTE WIN £10.10; PL £2.30, £1.50, £1.20; EX £39.40; CSF £31.60
TRIFECTA £132.50
DBI (SP%) L [Stalls 1-3] 55 (25%) M [4-9] 50 (44%) H [10-12] 45 (31%)

Image 011.

the only front runner in the race and drawn 12 on the favoured side of the track. Unquestionably she, together with the pace runners, would set it up for the hold-up horses, leaving Clifford Lee as much room as he wanted to get a pitch from stall four across to the favoured rail, settling behind the pace. Which was exactly how it panned out, with Fast Response winning easily by 2 lengths in front of Tahrib and Art Power in 3rd. I played quite heavily on the winner at 9/1 and saved stake on the second just in case.

To recap on that race, I should point out that the very obvious pace taking place on the stand rail would never be sustained, and the only way the pace runners in stalls 1, 2 and 3 could possibly survive to the line was by steering a straight course down the middle of the track, saving as much ground as possible, as they indeed did.

But whatever the jockeys'

89

decisions with their mounts were, they always had the hold-up horses to contend with in the latter part of the race, which is difficult to near-impossible in conditions like that.

I make no apologies for going on about the draw and the pace for horse racing on the flat, because it is fundamental in winner finding, and one or two of you will be slightly unsure on my instructions, so I am going to show you a table (image 013) and explain exactly the way I do it myself.

I generally use a plain sheet of paper and put the stall numbers left to right, or right to left in this instance, where stall one is on the far side.

The race I have chosen is a 5-furlong sprint at Thirsk, late April 2023 (see image 012). A class 3 handicap for 3-year-olds, with good prize money, and good ground forecast. There was, however, an overnight deluge, with 10ml rain significantly altering the ground to soft and, more importantly, the draw, making this near-side rail at Thirsk a premium for all jockeys as proved in the first two races, so it was no big surprise to see the higher numbers offered at lower odds. This shows how crucial the draw can be in situations like this, so always take note when ground-changing conditions occur.

THE METHOD

2.00 Best Odds Guaranteed Daily At **RTV**
Vickers.Bet Handicap (Class 3)
RACE 3 Winner £9,720 **5f**

£18,000 Total Race Value **For** 3yo Rated 71-90 (also open to such horses rated 91 and 90; such horses rated 70 and below are also eligible - see Standard Conditions) **Weights** highest weight 9st 9lb **Minimum Weight** 8-4 **Penalties** after April 15th, each race won 6lb **Clearpoint's Handicap Mark** 91 **Entries** 18 pay £90 **Penalty value 1st** £9,720 **2nd** £4,563 **3rd** £2,282.40 **4th** £1,141.20 DRAW ADVANTAGE: SLIGHT HIGH

1 (6) 1108- **CLEARPOINT** 177 D1 F1 — Hc1 b c Ardad-Pigeon Point — Richard Fahey Sheikh Rashid Dalmook Al Maktoum — 3 9-10 Oisin Orr (97)

2 (11) 33190- **REDEMPTION TIME** 247 D1 F1 — Hc1 b g1 Harry Angel-Red Box — Clive Cox Atlantic Equine — 3 9-10 Adam Kirby (90)

3 (2) 41223- **WASHINGTON HEIGHTS** 203 D1 F1 — Hc1 b g Washington Dc-Epping Rose — Kevin Ryan Hambleton Racing Ltd XXVII — 3 9-9 Tom Eaves (99)

4 (5) 101353- **STAR OF LADY M** 236 D4 S2 F1 — gr f Havana Grey-Abraj Dubai — David O'Meara M Madden — 3 9-7 Jason Watson (96)

5 (9) 324443- **NORTHCLIFF** (IRE) 247 — ch g1 Dandy Man-Colgin — Tim Easterby S Bulmer, P Hebdon & R Taylor — 3 9-6 David Allan (98)

6 (10) 8-63132 **DEMOCRACY DILEMMA** (IRE) 15 D2 S1 — b g Cotai Glory-Majestic Alexander — David Evans K McCabe — v 3 9-4 1 Hollie Doyle (99)

7 (13) 391- **SEANTRABH** (IRE) 179 D1 S1 — Hc1 b g1 Tasleet-Hot Stone — Declan Carroll Brian Chambers — 3 9-3 Harrison Shaw (98)

8 (4) 51920- **CAN TO CAN** (IRE) 218 D1 F1 — Hc1 b f Kodiac-Ridge Ranger — Adrian Nicholls1 B R Hirst — 3 9-1 Ben Curtis (99)

9 (14) 443027- **JM JUNGLE** (IRE) 218 D1 — b g1 Bungle Inthejungle-The Chew — John Quinn MPS Racing Ltd & The Ayrshire Tradesmen — 3 8-13 Jason Hart (97)

10 (12) 53212-3 **THANKUAPPRECIATE** 10 — b g Fountain Of Youth-Illusions — Nigel Tinkler Ms Sara Hattersley, And Miss Tracey Mann — 3 8-13 Rowan Scott (96)

11 (3) 318- **SECRET GUEST** 189 D1 — Hc1 gr g1 Havana Grey-Lady Macduff — Bryan Smart The Unscrupulous Judges — 3 8-13 1 Paul Mulrennan (101)

12 (8) 22213- **SPARKLING RED** (IRE) 235 BF CD1 — Hc1 b f Bungle Inthejungle-Hint Of Red — Michael Dods R Saunders,G Thompson,I Davison — 3 8-11 Connor Beasley (96)

13 (1) 18212- **MISS BRAZEN** 267 BF F2 CD1 — Hc1 b f Brazen Beau-Oui Je Affaire — Michael & David Easterby1 D & R Chapman, W&j Tinning & C Wallis — 3 8-9 1 Joanna Mason (97)

14 (7) 77-1 **WINTER CROWN** 58 D1 — Hc1 b Invincible Spirit-Berengaria — Julie Camacho2 Martin Hughes — 3 8-6 Graham Lee (93)

2022 (9 ran) Edward Cornelius (5) Keith Dalgleish 3 9-4 7/1 Callum Rodriguez OR85

BETTING FORECAST: 4 Washington Heights, **8** Clearpoint, Democracy Dilemma, Secret Guest, **9** Northcliff, **10** Redemption Time, Seantrabh, Star Of Lady M, Winter Crown, **12** Sparkling Red, Thankuappreciate, **14** Miss Brazen, **20** Jm Jungle, **33** Can To Can.

Image 012.

Democracy dilemma wins, ridden by Hollie Doyle, one of the best front running jockeys in the business. Another great Method result

91

So, for me, the key here with these young horses was draw and pace.

As you can see with the image, I have produced from my original draw jottings, stalls 13, 10, and 8 were front-runners amongst hold-up horses, with Seantrabh stall 13 heavily backed from 10s tissue to 9/2 and Thankuappreciate stall 12 12/1 tissue to 5/1.

This situation is great proof of me stating that you cannot use the **Method** blindly. The betting says these two horses are off, but simple investigation tells you otherwise.

Seantrabh had won his last race 179 days ago on soft beating (Tephi) a horse that had not achieved a R/P figure higher than 75. Along with every other runner in that last race with ratings even lower? Seantrabh clearly beat trees.

Thankuappreciate, however, had much better figures on soft and good to soft, but winning at 6 furlongs? And being a hold-up horse made it difficult for him here.

(I would like you to watch the replay of this race, showing how vigorous the jockey was on Thankuappreciate, and so very hard at work on his mount all through the race, eventually taking charge of all the other 5-furlong horses in this race except the winner.)

Democracy Dilemma, on the other hand, had very good figures with both wins achieved over 5 furlongs, had contested 6- and 7-furlong races so stamina would hold, and importantly a front-runner with one of the best front-running jockeys, Hollie Doyle in the saddle. I could not find anything else of interest in the race and bet quite heavily at 6/1 (tissue 8/1). Hollie rode to perfection, never to be caught, and returned 9/2 favourite and with another **Method** winner nicely in the book.

For explanation purposes this section is probably the most significant in the book, and I want you to not only spend some time absorbing this, I even urge you to read it over again and implant it with your way of approach to the betting and gambling structure you are now creating for yourself.

DRAW	14	13	12	11	10	9	8	7	6	5	4	3	2	1
RUNNING STYLE		L	H	H	L		L				H			
TISSUE	20	10	12	10	8	9	12	10	8	10	20	8	4	14
1ST SHOW	22	9/2	5	9	7	16	20	N/R	7	17/2	25	15/2	13/2	25
2ND SHOW	18	5	6	17/2	6	20	16		7	12	28	17/2	7	33
3RD SHOW	20	5	6	17/2	5	20	16		7	12	28	17/2	7	33
POST TIME	20	5	6	17/2	9/2	20	16		7	12	28	17/2	7	33
RESULT	3	4	2	10	1	6	11		5	12	13	8	9	7

Image 013

To explain the layout in the table (image 013), the 14 stall numbers go from left to right, followed by the front runners marked L.

Next, I include the hold-up runners in the race marked H.

Obviously, the remaining numbers although not marked are the runners who like to keep up with the pace (P).

Under that I jot all the tissue prices, under the draw numbers. (Careful not to mix them with race card numbers).

Number 14 drawn 7 was a 10/1 non-runner and therefore reducing tissue prices slightly. Everything at this point was in-keeping with a run-of-the-mill horse race that happens every day...That is, until the next step in our winner-finding **Method** showed its head, and the excitement bells began to ring.

The late morning show, as discussed, was informative, with nearside draw number prices reduced and low draw numbers in general drifting. I now have in front of me a truly clear picture beginning to form.

Parade time and post-time prices I have included as they happened.

Armed with what you have absorbed with this book, this simple exercise is now exciting stuff unfolding in front of you. No guessing, just solid information to fill your boots.

Looking closely at the overall picture that I have created with little effort, the **Method** gave you the top 5 drawn horses including the winner, 2nd, 3rd, and 4th – a visual that I want you to create for yourself that contains that important edge we all search for when gambling. Remember, I am only highlighting one particular race. I can bore you senseless with hundreds of similar races that you will find easy to assess for yourself with the **Method** applied correctly.

Let us now look closely at the prices from the value-seeker's prospective

Draw 1 Tissued at 14/1 could be backed at 33/1

Draw 2, 4/1 to 7/1

Draw 3, 8/1 to 17/2

Draw 4, 20/1 to 28/1

And so on.

And now look at the result across the bottom of the table. Plenty to feel good about with those prices before the race, though little to shout about afterwards.

My final point on the draw where the bias is well known, I find it worth paying attention and taking note of a horse being backed against the bias. Not to say you should back them particularly, we must stick to our guns, but they sometimes prove bulletproof and well worth following in future races. Put them in your notebook – just a small tip.

ALL-WEATHER

I suspect another book can be written on all-weather racing with the various tracks that all have their individual racing patterns. The **Method** can be very rewarding with all-weather racing, and A/W racing can often be described as pretty specialist.

Thousands of the serious form students only bet on the all-weather and make a living doing so, and in many ways, it becomes reflected in the **Method**.

First introduced to the UK in 1989 after severe winter weather conditions stopped so much racing on turf, the all-weather racing kept the industry alive and became very popular with trainers and punters alike and, as I have just highlighted, many of whom still consider it to be somewhat easier in assessing form.

Artificial racing, as we first knew it, was to become a saviour for the bookmaking industry, giving everyone hope for racing to continue all year round. Even though we still see abandonments in severe weather, it became a big success, and is now here to stay.

Polytrack are the company to proclaim their product to be the best, which rides similar to good turf ground, and closely followed by Tapeta, another company who provide synthetic surfaces for flat racing.

Six tracks have regular all-weather race meetings, namely…

Chelmsford, Kempton, and Lingfield, all run on Polytrack surfaces.

Wolverhampton, Newcastle, and Southwell run on Tapeta surfaces.

From a betting perspective there is little or no advantage with the two surfaces, but very interesting differences to be considered with the different tracks.

Lingfield is tight and undulating and the draw is very important here, especially on the 1 mile 2-furlong course that has a tight turn just after the start. The jockey needs to settle the mount if drawn wide and drop in behind or sprint to the bend and get an early position, but that depends on the running style of that horse, which is where the pdf sheet is important in assessing the pace. If a horse misses the break he or she will struggle to get into the race, on the varying left turns, and Lingfield's short straight, whereas at Southwell the jockey can sit and wait for the much longer 3-furlong straight to make his finishing move, and note how the jocks use the width of the track at Southwell as the race unfolds on that final burst. Hard to achieve at Lingfield, where they can become stuck outside on the hare rail.

The 5-furlong and 6-furlong races at Lingfield's all-weather track can often suit a horse that is quick from the gate and leads, but always beware of the fast finishers who have been locked up behind for most of the race. It will not happen like that at Southwell because the 5-furlong track is straight, and those that sprint away at Lingfield and win, find it altogether different to achieve the same at Southwell. Use the replays and take advantage of what the different tracks will supply. Essentially, I am telling you to note the running styles at the all-weather tracks with horses on and off the bridle on the tight track and not being able to gallop, yet at Southwell and Newcastle they can.

Kempton all-weather track is the only right-handed one of the six and has a cutaway in the straight about 2 furlongs from home, that benefits the hold-up horses who make a move on the inside. There are 2 tracks at Kempton which are effectively a track within a track, making the inside loop that much tighter.

The 5-furlong course is probably the tightest if not the fastest in the country and an inside draw is very favourable, although very few 5-furlong races are run here. But again, take time to check the running style of the horse because the opposite will occur if your selection does not get a break and gets boxed inside with nowhere to go. The 1 mile 2-furlong races are run on the inner loop at Kempton and front runners fare pretty well.

The 6-furlong and to some extent 7-furlong races run on the outer track mostly prove to favour an inside pitch, but they are always overbet, so search for the power pack finisher who often comes late and spoils the party, and watch closely the betting patterns, especially with late money. The **Method** should give good indication with these races, and often does, and whilst I recommend you to pay respect to a solid **Method** horse, the rule of thumb with most all-weather races is caution, because they are generally poor quality events with lower-rated animals taking on lower-rated animals, and it is this type of horse who is not the most reliable.

I have had some rather good touches, it is fair to say, mainly when a horse constantly struggles to get a clear run and is then unleashed at Southwell or Newcastle where he or she can show his stride and pace.

Wolverhampton and Chelmsford are much of a muchness all-weather racecourse. Both oblong in shape, with little to be gleaned except for the starting points, where positions vary on both tracks. They both ride similar, though different jockeys have their own opinions on how to ride them, whether to breakfast from a wide draw and then slow the pace or go hell for leather from the gate in sprints, so I recommend you check the starting positions of the track in question, all of which can be found in the R/P or the web site, and of course never overlook the draw, and the running styles, before making your decisions to bet, especially if you are serious about betting on all-weather racing.

Newcastle all-weather course looks like a golf club if you look at the layout from an aerial view. Famous for having the only straight all-weather mile course in the world, Newcastle is a great test and a very fair track. Horses can often be affected by a strong cross wind there, causing them to be unbalanced, so it is recommended not to be too quick off the blocks until you check it out, but generally speaking most horses act on the track, and don't be put off by front runners, they surprisingly have a good strike rate here.

I have learnt that the track at Newcastle can ride different meeting to meeting, when it often pays to watch the bias unfold on the first few races and use the draw accordingly on the remainder of the card. They can often win stands-side here, race after race, and then at the next meeting the jocks prefer to run down the middle, completely ignoring the nearside rail.

My final advice for all-weather racing is to check out trainers and jockey strike rates, that are clear indication to the running and training programmes of certain stables and their jockeys who achieve regular success at these tracks.

The last and important tip I want to give you relates to staking. I never want you to feel so good about winning that you lose sight of money itself. That may well seem a brash statement, but we can all do it when gambling. Do not sit there looking at yesterday's winning balance and steam in on some selection with the comfort of...'If it loses, I can afford it.' You cannot, today is a new day with new profits to achieve. So, take the tip and do what I have got used to doing.

Stake smaller than you would normally do and gradually work on your winning day, trying to get a stake that will give you confidence in going for that larger bet. In other words, bet with the profit of the day. If it does not happen early in your day, you can never risk a large bet and you will never lose a large chunk of your betting balance. There is always another day, and **never, ever** steam into those short price, odds-on favourites that are being hammered in the market, and become a member of the bookies' benefit club. You will lose many more than you win and, although sounding hypercritical to the **Method,** this type of gambling is **forbidden** in my class, and "picking up money off the floor" is one of the oldest statements in gambling, and other overused clichés such as 'it's a certainty', 'cannot get beat', 'will win pulling a cart', are to be ignored.

My brother has some useless clichés he uses such as

"none so dark as those that cannot see."

Or "It's all water over the bridge." They too are better unsaid.

The information and supporting races I have described for you throughout this book could not all happen in one day or one week, it has happened over time, but please do not think they are odd happenings that form the contents of this book. They are mostly drawn from memos and files that I have documented for my own benefit of which I have found a way to share with you.

These happenings with horse-racing are regular and daily occurrences that will continue to happen as long as the sport exists.

I trust you have found interest in what you have read, as much as I have had spelling it out for you.

As I mentioned in the foreword, all the descriptions can be checked out now that you are hopefully subscribed to the Racing Post, under the archive section of back issues.

Please pace yourself slowly at first and give yourself time to apply the **Method** correctly. You will not only enjoy your racing much more, but you are also now armed with a whole new understanding of the horse racing world which in turn will achieve financial rewards that will alter your approach to gambling and, importantly, winning.

GOOD LUCK

It is always good to close with a success story, and none better than a mention for a good friend of mine, Tony Elliot, who set up a very successful racing syndicate and has been grinding winners from a different perspective to that of the Method, although several of their recent winners fit into the Method bracket quite nicely. But there was more than a ray of sunshine for the members when Rogue Millennium won the Duke of Cambridge Stakes at Royal Ascot, for the Rogues Gallery Syndicate.

Unfortunately I was not there on the day but still soaked up the atmosphere somehow from home, and I met with Tony, his trainer, Tom Clover, his trainer's wife Jackie, and one of the members for lunch in the owners and trainers bar at Ascot the next day, for a second celebration, and I asked Tony to maybe spell out how the operation works for the benefit of my reader. Who knows? Some of you may fancy a dabble yourselves.

Tom, Tony, Tom and Jackie Clover

TONY WRITES

Rogues Gallery Racing was set up by Mr Tony Elliott. The name came from six very disgruntled racehorse owners who were finding it hard to get any value in this sport of kings. After exploring every avenue and finding absolutely no value, they decided to go it alone; this was in 2020.

6 people from all walks of life came together and the "Rogues" were created. It was all a bit tongue-in-cheek; we loved our racing, and we loved a gamble.

This has now been moulded into our own business model and after 3 years and a lot of learning we now have over 300 members and over 30 horses. There is no profit made from our members and all horses and training bills are split equally. We only buy horses with scope and pedigree, and work hard with our very trustworthy trainer, Tom Clover. Trust is a very hard thing to find in horse racing but the team we have put together for trust and value is second to none and our unique set-up is unlike any other syndicate of this size.

We are highly successful; in the three and a half years we have been going we have won over half a million in prize money.

Our biggest success to date is Rogue Millennium, who won a Group 2 at Royal Ascot and is about to go for a Group 1 in France. Hopefully, she will be sold at Christmas for a few million and we can move the syndicate to another level.

We also like a bet and when you are in control it makes it easier to beat the bookies and we do that on a regular basis, which really helps on paying the bills.

In only three and a half years we have had many nice horses that have taken us to a lot of places, even abroad. It has been an incredible journey, a trip of a lifetime and fantastic value. We have been playing at the very top of a normally very expensive sport.

Before going to print, Rogue Millennium contested a 4 hundred-thousand-pound group one race at Leopardstown finishing second.

Well done her!

Look us up at Roguesgalleryracing.com for full transparency. We are the team.

The author